EGYPTIAN HISTORICAL RECOI OF THE LATER EIGHTEENTH DYNASTY

TRANSLATED INTO ENGLISH
by

Barbara Cumming

FROM THE ORIGINAL HIEROGLYPHIC TEXT AS PUBLISHED IN
W. HELCK, '*URKUNDEN DER 18. DYNASTIE*', HEFT 17–19
With Reference to Professor Helck's German Translation

***FASCICLE 3

ARIS & PHILLIPS Ltd – WARMINSTER – ENGLAND

British Library Cataloguing in Publication Data

Egyptian historical records of the late eighteenth dynasty
Fasc. 3
1. Egypt - History - Eighteenth dynasty,
ca. 1570-1320 B.C. - Sources
I. Cumming, Barbara
932'.014 DT87

Printed and Published by Aris & Phillips Ltd, Warminster, Wiltshire, England

ISBN 0 85668 284 5

CONTENTS - Fascicle III

486. Granite Stela of Tuthmosis IV, found in front of the Sphinx at Gizeh 1539a

(Vyze Operations carried on at the Pyramids of Gizeh III pl.B, p.115, Lepsius Denkm. III 68; Young Hieroglyphics, pl.80: Brugsch ZÄS 14,89; Erman Sitzungsbericht Preussische Akademie der Wissenschaft. 1904,428 ff: coll. with the original.

Description:

The device at the head of the stela shows no unusual features. The scene in the upper part of the stela shows two opposing images of the king offering to the sphinx, who is recumbent upon a pedestal.

Inscriptions on the right:

The king: The king of Upper and Lower Egypt, lord of the Two Lands, Menkheperurē', Tuthmosis, gleaming-of-diadems, given life.

The sphinx: Ḥarmachis.

The scene: Offering incense and cool water.

Speech of the sphinx: Words to be spoken: I have given life and dominion to the lord of the Two Lands, Tuthmosis, gleaming-of-diadems.

Inscriptions on the left:

The king: The king of Upper and Lower Egypt, lord of the Two Lands, Menkheperurē', Tuthmosis, gleaming-of-diadems, given life, stability and dominion like Rē'.

The sphinx: Ḥarmachis.

The scene: Paying (one's) respects with a *nmst*-vessel.

Speech of the sphinx:

Words to be spoken: I have given might to the lord of the Two Lands, Tuthmosis, gleaming-of-diadems.

The central vertical band of hieroglyphs reads thus:

Words to be spoken: I have caused Menkheperurē' to appear on the throne of Geb, Tuthmosis, gleaming-of-diadems in the office of Atum.

Principal Inscriptions: 15

Regnal year 1, month 3 of the Inundation, day 9 under the Majesty of Horus, "Mighty bull, perfect-of-diadems", Two Ladies, "Stable in kingship like Atum", "Golden Horus", the strong of might, who fends off the Nine Bows", king of Upper and Lower Egypt, Menkheperurē', son of Rē', Tuthmosis, gleaming-of-diadems, beloved of Harmachis, given life, stability and dominion like Rē', for ever.

(Long) live the good god, the son of Atum, protector of Ḥarakhty, the living image of the lord of all, a sovereign created by Rē', potent heir of Khepery*, beautiful of countenance like his father, who came forth perfect, equipped with his Horus form as his firstborn, king of Upper and Lower Egypt, beloved of the gods, possessor of graciousness among the Ennead, who purifies Heliopolis and propitiates Rē', who rehabilitates the temple of Ptaḥ, who offers (the image of) Ma'ēt to Atum and presents her to the one South of his Wall, who erects monuments as a daily offering to Horus who made all that exists, who seeks out things of benefit for the gods of Upper and Lower Egypt, who builds their temples of limestone and renews their offering loaves, the son of Atum of his body, Tuthmosis, gleaming-of-diadems, like Rē', heir of Horus upon his throne, Menkheperurē', given life.

Now his Majesty was a royal child like the child Horus 15
on Chemmis*, his beauty being like the protector of his father. Men regarded him as they did the god himself, one for the love of whom the army rejoiced, whilst all the royal children and officials were under the sway of his might and subject to his youthful vigour, when he underwent his rebirth*, his strength being like that of the son of Nut.

It was in the desert of Memphite nome on its southern and northern side that he would pursue his leisure taking recreation, shooting at a target of copper and hunting lions and game whilst travelling on his chariot, his horses being fleeter than the wind, together with one of his retainers, without any man being aware of it.

Now the time came for granting rest to his attendant near to the outstanding monument of Ḥarmachis* which is near to (the cult place) of Sokar in Rosetau, to Renenutet in
Ta-Mut* in the pyramid plateau, /to Mut, the lady of the 1542
northern wall and the southern wall, to Sekhmet, pre-eminent in the desert, Seth, the oldest magiician of the hallowed place of the first time in the neighbourhood of the lord of Kher'aḥa*, and of the sacred way of the gods of the horizon west of Heliopolis.

Now the image of Khepery, the most great, rested in this place, the great of power and holy in awe, the shade of Rē' having alighted on it. The estates of Memphis and every town which is near to it come to him, their arms (raised) in adoration before him, bearing a large pile of offerings for his ka.

One of these days it so happened that the king's son, Tuthmosis, came along in order to travel around at the time of midday. He sat down in the shadow of this great god and sleep took him at the moment when the sun was at his zenith. He found the Majesty of this august god speaking with his own mouth as a father speaks to his son saying, "Look at me, regard me, my son, Tuthmosis! I am your father, Ḥarmachis-Rē-Atum who has given you kingship upon earth at the head of the
living/. You shall wear the White Crown and the Red Crown 1543
on the throne of Geb, the prince*. You own the land in its length and breadth, (all) that which the Eye of the Lord of All illumines, the sustenance from within the earth is in your keeping and the abundant tribute of all foreign lands and a lifetime (consisting of a great span of years."

"My face is turned towards you, even my heart (also). You are mine. See my condition resembles that of someone in extremity for every limb of mine is dismembered. The desert sand on which I am is encroaching on me (yet) I have waited in order to let you do that which is in my heart for I know that you are my son and my protector. Come nearer; see, I am with you! I am your guide!" (Thus) be brought his words to an end.

Thereupon this king's son stared astonished when he heard these words................he understood the words of this god, but he put silence in his heart, saying:/
Come, let us go to our house in the city that we may set 154
aside offerings for this god and that we may bring to him oxen, herbage, and all (kinds of) plants, and that we may give praise to those who were aforetime................. the august goddess...........Kha'frē', the perfect one whom Atum and Rē-Ḥarakhty created, Rē'Harmachis.......... ....at the festivals of...............all.........being numerous........................for my Majesty for causing to live who......................for Khepery in the western horizon of Heliopolis in.........................(the rest has broken away.)

Footnotes to 486

1540.9 Symbol of the rising sun in the form of a dung beetle. Also a symbol of the emergent deity Atum, as creator. (Rundle Clark Myth and Symbol in Ancient Egypt, p.40 ff.)

1540.15 The presentation of a small squatting image of Ma'ēt represented the maintenance of universal order.

1541.1 The "Swamp of the Bee King" where Isis took refuge with Horus from the fury of Seth and whence he set out to protect his father and settle with his adversary. (PT 1214b ff. Rundle Clark Myth and Symbol in Ancient Egypt p.186 foll.)

1541.6 wḥm.n.f snw. f Lit: repeated his circuit, i.e. was reborn like the young sun.

1541.16 The sphinx at Gizeh.

1541.18 This is believed by Helck to be a primeval hill bearing the same name as the primeval hill in the small temple of Medinet Habu. (Helck Übersetzung p.141, n.11.)

1542.5 The sphinx at Gizeh.

Footnotes to 486 contd.

1543.1 According to Helck a designation which relates to Geb as heir of Atum. iry-p't is the name for the prince of most senior rank who performed the administrative tasks which at the end of the Third Dynasty were assumed by the Vizier. (Helck Ubersetzung p.142, n.5.)

487. Report concerning the Nubian Campaign of Tuthmosis IV which took place in his Eighth Year, from a Rock Stela at Konosso 1545

(de Morgan Cat. Mon. 1 p.66, coll. Abel 1909)

(Long) live Horus "Mighty bull, perfect-of-diadems", Two Ladies, "Stable of kingship, like Atum", Golden Horus, "Great of strength, who fends off the Nine Bows", king of Upper and Lower Egypt, Menkheperurē', given life for ever.

Regnal year 9, month 3 of winter, day 2. Now his Majesty was in the Southern City in the area of Karnak, his hands being pure with the purity of a god, having propitiated his father Amun, since he had granted to him an eternity as king and infinite time established upon the throne of Horus.

Someone came in order to say to his Majesty, "A Nubian has descended upon the district of Wawat, having planned rebellion against Egypt. He is gathering to himself all the reprobate foreigners and rebels of another land."

The king proceeded in peace to the temple in the morning and had a large pile of offerings presented to his father who had created his beauty. His Majesty made petition in person in the presence of the ruler of gods, taking counsel with him concerning the manner of the campaign so that he would inform
him about that which would happen to him./ He guided him on 1546
a path of success in order to do that which his ka desired, as when a father speaks to his son whom he has begotten, since his seed is in him.

It was with joyful heart that he left him. He ordered that his army be mustered immediately and sent it out in bravery and strength. Thereafter his Majesty set out in order to overthrow him who had attacked him in the land of Nubia, being valiant in his ship of gold like Rē' when he goes aboard the night barque, its sail being composed of red and green linen (with) the chariotry in ranks escorting him, his army being (also) with him, the experienced soldiers* being in two rows with the recruits at their side and the fleet ready with its crews. The king travelled southwards like Orion having illumined Upper Egypt with his beauty. The men shouted for joy for love of him and the women became excited at the news. Month in Armant was the protection of his body, his Uraeus was his guide before him, every god of Upper Egypt held a bouquet to his nose/.

Nekhbet of El-kab* set the insignia of my Majesty in 154
place, her hands clasping the sceptre and binding together the Nine Bows for me. It so happened that I was celebrating the time of the festival of Washing the Image having stopped in the town of Beḥdet.

The good god came forth like Month in all his forms, equipped with his weapons of war, raging like Seth, the Ombite, with the sun behind him with life unfailing and no night on the mountains, together with every single brave warrior in his retinue, without delay.

His army came to him. He wreaked much slaughter by means of his valiant might, the fear of him having entered every body, for it was throughout the world that Rē' had instilled the fear of him like (that of) Sekhmet in a year of plague. He was watchful and did not sleep. He traversed the eastern desert opening the ways like the Upper Egyptian jackal, seeking out the trail of him who had attacked him. He found all the
Nubian foe in a concealed valley/ of which no-one was aware 154
since it was hidden from men behind the mountains. He..... far from......then he removed the settlement together with their inhabitants, their cattle and all their property which was in their keeping. (The rest of the inscription is illegible.)

Footnotes to 487

1546.11 Lit: the "strong of arm", a word which normally means "adult". Hence the translation "experienced soldiers" in contrast to recruits.

1547.1 Vulture goddess who together with cobra goddess Wadjet protected the king.

488. Inscription of Tuthmosis IV on the Lateran Obelisk which Tuthmosis III had left unfinished

(Marucchi Gli. obelischi egiziane di Roma pls. 1/11.)

Description:

Each set of inscriptions is surmounted by a rectangular frame showing the king kneeling and offering to Amun.

Inscription on the northern side, on the right: 1549

The good god, "Perfect-of-diadems, stable of kingship like Atum, the strong in might, who fends off the Nine Bows, king of Upper and Lower Egypt, Menkheperurē, who seizes by means of his might like the lord of Thebes*, great of strength like Month, whose victory over all foreign lands Amun has granted, and to whom unknown lands come with the fear of him in their bodies, the son of Rē', Tuthmosis, gleaming-of-diadems, beloved of Amun-Rē', bull of his mother, given life.

Inscription on the southern side, on the right:

The son of Rē', Tuthmosis, gleaming-of-diadems. He has raised it up (the obelisk) in Karnak, making his obelisk in fine gold, the beauty of which has illumined Thebes, being engraven with the name of his father, the good god Menkheperurē'. The king of Upper and Lower Egypt, Menkheperurē', beloved of Rē', did this in order to cause the name of his father to remain and to endure in the temple of Amun-Rē'. Thus the son of Rē', Tuthmosis, gleaming of diadems, given life for ever, acted for his benefit.

Inscription on the southern side, on the left: 1550

The king of Upper and Lower Egypt, lord of action, Menkheperurē, begotten-of-Re'. Now it was his Majesty who had a single, very great obelisk, which the king of Upper and Lower Egypt, Menkheperurē, had brought, embellished at the hands of craftsmen after his Majesty had found this obelisk, after it had spent thirty-five years lying on its side on the southern side of Karnak. My father commanded me to raise it for him, for I am his son and his protector.

Inscription on the western side, on the right:

The king of Upper and Lower Egypt, Menkheperurē', whom Amun has chosen from among mankind, born...........whom he (loves) more than any other king. It is inasmuch as he holds him dear that he rejoices on beholding his beauty. He has placed the inhabitants of the south in his charge and the inhabitants of the north come bowing before his power. He made it as his monument for his father Amun-Rē', raising for him a very large obelisk at the upper gate-way of Karnak opposite Thebes. Thus the son of Rē', his beloved, given life, acted for his benefit.

Inscription on the western side, on the left: 155

The king of Upper and Lower Egypt, Menkheperurē', the eldest son, serviceable to him who begat him, who makes the lord of gods content because he knows the excellence of his designs. He it is who leads him to the ways of good fortune and binds the Nine Bows for him under his sandals. Now his Majesty.........being attentive with regard to the establishment of the monuments of his father, the king himself giving the directive, the ingenious one like him South of his Wall. He raised it in the space of a moment and delighted the heart of him who created him, the son of Rē', Tuthmosis, gleaming-of-diadems, given life.

Inscription on the eastern side, on the right:

The good god, strong of might, sovereign who conquers by means of his strength, who instils dread of himself among the Bedouin and sends out* his war-cry among the tribesmen of Nubia. His father Amun nurtured him, in order that he should exercise an enduring kingship, whilst the chieftains of all foreign lands bow before the power of his Majesty, who speaks with his mouth and acts with his arms. All
that which he has commanded comes to pass,/ the king of 155
Upper and Lower Egypt, Menkheperurē', whose name is enduring in Karnak, given life.

Inscription on the eastern side, on the left:

The king of Upper and Lower Egypt, Menkheperurē', who embellishes monuments in Karnak, with gold, lapis lazuli, turquoise and all (kinds of) precious stones and the great barque on the river, Amenuserḥet, with new 'š - wood which his Majesty felled in the foreign land of Retjenu, it being (also) covered in its length with gold, with all its decorations having been fashioned anew in order to (convey) the beauty of his father, Amun, during his triumphal procession on the river. Thus the son of Rē', Tuthmosis, gleaming-of-diadems, given life, acted for his benefit.

Inscription on the southern side of the Pyramidion:

The king of Upper and Lower Egypt, Menkheperurē', given life, beloved of Amun-Rē', lord of the thrones of the Two Lands and lord of heaven.

Inscription on the southern side, above the vertical lines:

The good god, Menkheperurē', son of Rē', Tuthmosis, given life like Rē', beloved of Amun-Rē', king of the gods.

Footnotes to 488

1548.13 Month.

1551.15 dỉ does not strictly mean "to send" but the latter seems to be the only reasonable word in this context since dỉ is more versatile in meaning than its English equivalents 'give' and 'place'.

489 Fragment of an Offering List from the reign of Tuthmosis IV in Karnak*

(Mariette Karnak, pl.33: de Rouge Inscript.hiérogl. 164; coll. with the original.)

.....................in large baking ratio for this temple in excess of what had been before. 1553

List of Offerings:

(Some lines are missing.)

sḫt-loaves	baking ratio*	10	quadruple ḥeḳat	2
sm3t-' loaves	baking ratio	10	quadruple ḥeḳat	2
tsrwt-loaves	baking ratio	30	quadruple ḥeḳat	2
bỉt-loaves (large)	baking ratio	10	quadruple ḥeḳat	20
bỉt-loaves (second quality)	baking ratio	20	quadruple ḥeḳat	40

Total of various loaves for the divine offering 155

beer 2 ds-jugs	baking ratio	4	quadruple ḥeḳat	4

together with giving to him one hin of wine from the jar
which his Majesty donated and one hin of milk from the divine offering,/ his meat offering being flesh from the flank........at every festival. (Rest of line empty) 155

In the presence of this image, the name of which is, "Menkheperurē' fends off the Nine Bows" in the course of every day.................in the presence of the other image of Osiris, king of Upper and Lower Egypt, Menkheperē', justified, which is beside it. Men shall give............ white bread and fruit, and men shall give the honey belonging to it from the treasury of Pharoah, LPH, and fruit........... of all the good and pure produce from Upper and Lower Egypt.. ....Amun and a ḥt-'3-goose from the estate of the superintendent of the treasury for the festival of the new moon...................on the morning of the Neḥeb-kau* festival. (Also) there was offered to him............from the fields of the divine offerings of Amun-Rē', five........ ....loaves and five snw-pots of honey from the treasury of Pharoah, LPH..............from among the booty of his Majesty in wretched Naharin on his first campaign of victory......... ....fresh land from the estate of him who made him.

It was in order that my statue might remain firm in..... 155
..........that my Majesty did this........beloved........... Amun-Rē' on the head, two tall plumes on the brow, being alive and stable in the palace, LPH..............enduring old age.. ....of my Majesty being established in the presence of my image for ever.

Footnotes to 489 See Urk IV 1552 for map.

1553.9 The flame sign is given in WB 1 552 as 'baking ratio'. In Urk IV 1798.3 the same is used to refer to beer. Evidently it indicated how much bread or beer could be made from a single oipe. (See also Urk IV 642 in the inscription of the High Steward Amenḥotp of Memphis, where the flame sign also refers to beer.)

1554.13 The first day of the first month of winter presided over by the snake demon Neḥeb-kau. (Frankfort Kingship and the Gods, p.103 ff.)

490 <u>Scene with Accompanying Inscriptions on a Rock Stela from Konosso</u>

(Lepsius Denkm. III 69e; Champollion Not. descr. 1, p.164.)

Description:

The king on the left, followed by the queen, smites two prisoners in the presence of two gods.

The king: Horus, mighty of arm, lord of action, king of Upper and Lower Egypt, Menkheperurē', son of Rē', Tuthmosis, gleaming-of-diadems.

The queen: The king's daughter and king's "sister", the great royal wife Wazet.

Two gods attend the ceremony:

1. Dedwen, pre-eminent in Nubia.

He says: I have given the tribesmen to you.

2. Kha, lord of the western desert.

He says: I have given to you every foreign land.

Principal inscription:

Horus, "Mighty bull, perfect-of-diadems, Two Ladies, "Stable of kingship like Atum", Golden Horus, "The strong of might who fends off the Nine Bows," /king of Upper and
Lower Egypt, Menkheperurē',son of Rē', Tuthmosis, gleaming- 1556
of-diadems, beloved of Amun-Rē', given life like Rē'. Regnal year 7, month 3 of winter, day 8...................

491 Inscriptions on Two Small Stela from the Mortuary Temple of Tuthmosis IV in Thebes

(Petrie Six Temples of Thebes, pl.1, Nos. 7 and 8.)

Description:

A· is a limestone stela (UC 14372); almost all the scene has been lost. B· is of sandstone.

Inscription accompanying the scene: Offering water.

A. Principal inscription:

The settlement of the fortress of Menkheperurē', among the Khorians*. The booty of his Majesty in the town of Ḳadjar.

B. Sandstone stela. The scene shows the king standing on left before a god.

The god is called:

Amun-Rē', lord of the thrones of the Two Lands.

The king is called:

The good god, Menkheperurē',given life.

Principal inscription:

The settlement of wretched Kush. That which his Majesty took in the course of his capture.

Footnote to 491

1556.10 The inhabitants of Palestine and Syria. (Gardiner AEO 1, p.180*)

492 Inscription of Tuthmosis IV on the Fourth Pylon in Karnak 1557

(Champollion Not. descr. II 131; coll. with the original.)

.................who takes thought for the future, who seeks out things of benefit for his father who placed him upon his throne, who makes his temple in which he has appeared in Karnak both lofty and broad as a monument for the lord of eternity in the place in which he has settled down, the son of Rē', Tuthmosis, gleaming-of-diadems, given life.

................it having been extended and greatly enlarged, more had been done by those aforetime, its extent being (so) vast that it reached to the sky and its radiance flooded the Two Lands. It made Karnak festive.

The southern part of Egypt rejoices at the sight of it................who created his beauty, Amun-Rē', king of the gods, who guides his Majesty towards carrying out for him everything which he wishes to occur, for it is as his protector that he has acknowledged him, one who rehabilitates his house of millions............the son of Rē', Tuthmosis, gleaming-of-diadems, for ever.

493 Inscription upon Black Granite Offering Table from Kom Azazieh near to Mitrahine 1558

(Kamal. Tables d'Offrandes p.72, No. 23088)

Inscription on the right:

(Long) live Horus, "Mighty bull, beloved of Thebes", Two Ladies, "Powerful-of-diadems in all lands", Golden Horus, "Stable of.........like Ḥarakhty", son of Rē', Tuthmosis, gleaming-of-diadems. He made it as his monument for his father, Ptaḥ, given life. Thus the good god, Menkheperurē', given life, stability and dominion like Rē', for ever, acted for his benefit.

Inscription on the left:

(Long) live Horus, "Mighty bull, perfect-of-diadems", Two Ladies, "Stable of kingship like Atum", Golden Horus, "The strong of might who fends off the Nine Bows", king of Upper and Lower Egypt, Menkheperurē'. He made it as his monument for his father, Ptaḥ, that he might celebrate a "gift of life" ceremony. Thus the son of Rē', his beloved, Tuthmosis, gleaming-of-diadems, given life like Rē' for ever, acted for him.

494 Inscriptions from the Chariot of Tuthmosis IV from his tomb 1559

(Carter-Newberry Tomb of Tuthmosis IV)

Description:

The scene accompanying section A. shows the king in his chariot shooting arrows at Syrians. The scene accompanying section B. is of a similar nature to A. The scene accompanying section C. shows the king as a sphinx trampling Syrians, whilst section D. contains a similar scene in which the king is trampling Nubians.

A. Inscription outside on the right:

The good god, beloved of Month, who is keen in all labour and valiant with his chariot team like Astarte*, strong of heart among the multitude, a possessor of might, lord of action, the good god, Menkheperurē', given life like Rē'.

Inscription behind the king:

The good god, ruler of Heliopolis, lord of the Two Lands, Tuthmosis, gleaming-of-diadems.

B. Inscription outside on the left:

The good god, the valiant and alert, the aggressive one without equal, who succeeds by means of his heroism more than that which the Two Lands can imagine and more than all the army can see together in a single place, the king of Upper and Lower Egypt, Menkheperurē',strong of might.

Inscription behind the king:

The good god, lord of the Two Lands, lord of action and possessor of might, Tuthmosis, gleaming-of-diadems, given life like Rē'.

C. Inscription on the inside on the left:

The good god, lord of the Two Lands, Menkeheperurē', son of Rē', his beloved, Tuthmosis, gleaming-of-diadems, given life like Rē', who tramples all the obscure foreign lands of the north.

The speech of Month who stands behind the king:

Words to be spoken. I have given to you bravery and strength against all foreign lands like one who loves you. Month-Rē', the great of strength, the Theban Horus who overthrows all the territories of all the Fenkhu.

D. Inscription on the inside on the right: (p.32.)

The king of Upper and Lower Egypt, Menkheperurē', son of Rē', Tuthmosis, gleaming-of-diadems, lord of might like Rē', who tramples all the territories of the foreign lands.

Speech of Month:

Words to be spoken: I have given to you might and power to trample the tribesmen in their habitations. Month, the lord of Thebes, who smites the Nubians and severs their noses.

List of conquered peoples as seen in the interior of the chariot:

On the left. Asiatics: Naharin, Sangar, Tunip, Shasu*, Kadesh, Tjeksy.

On the right. Nubians; '3 Kurja, Miuy, Irem, Gerses, Tiurek.

Footnotes to 494

1559.6 A goddess of Syrian origin. Introduced in the Eighteenth Dynasty.

1560.15 A general name for Asiatic Bedouins. (Gardiner AEO 1, p.1, 93*)

495 Inscription on a Small Pink Granite Obelisk from Aswan 1561

(Küntz, Obelisques pl.X, No. 17016)

...............son of Rē', Tuthmosis, gleaming-of-diadems. He made it as his monument for his father Khnum, making for him two altar obelisks. May he celebrate a "gift of life" ceremony eternally.

496 Inscriptions on Blocks from the Temple of Trajan in Elephantine

(de Morgan Cat. Mon. p.115.)

The king of Upper and Lower Egypt, Menkheperurē'

son of Rē', Tuthmosis, gleaming-of-diadems. He made it as his monument for his father Khnum.................

497 Inscription from a Fragment of a Limestone Statue which was found to the South of the Ninth Pylon in Karnak

(Habachi *Ann. Serv.* 38p. 80/3, coll.)

The good god, lord of action..........Menkheperurē' ....It was his Majesty who embellished this monument for his father, 'Akheperurē'.

The queen stood to the left:

The great royal wife, mistress of the Two Lands, the king's mother..............

498 Foundation Deposits of Tuthmosis IV from the Temple of Ptaḥ at Memphis

(Petrie *Memphis* I, pl.19.)

A. The good god, Menkheperurē', beloved of Ptaḥ.

B. Son of Rē', Tuthmosis, gleaming-of-diadems, beloved of Ptaḥ.

499 Inscription on a Piece of Ivory Inlay from a Throne from Amarna

(Borchardt *MDOG* 55, pl.5.)

Description: The scene shows the king smiting a prisoner in the presence of a falcon-headed god.

The king: Menkheperurē', Tuthmosis, gleaming-of-diadems.

The speech of the god: Take to yourself the battleaxe, O good god, that you may smite the chieftains of all foreign lands.

500 Inscription from a Small Limestone Stela from the Temple of the Sphinx

Hölscher, Grabdenkmal des Königs Chefren. Pl 161

Description: The device at the head of the stela shows no unusual features.

The king: The good god, Menkheperurē', son of Rē', Tuthmosis, gleaming-of-diadems.

The queen: The great royal wife, Nefertere.

The goddess: Mut, who is in front of the "horns of the gods"*

Footnote to 500

1562.16 Helck believes this to be a locality in the region of Gizeh. (Übersetzung p.151, n.1.)

501 Upper Part of a Stela from Seriaqus

(Junker MDIK 1 28.)

Description:

Scene A. on the left shows the king making offering to Atum. Scene B. on the right shows the king making offering to Rē'-Ḥarakhty.

A. The king of Upper and Lower Egypt, lord of action, Menkheperurē', given life, like Rē' for ever.

The scene is described thus: Offering š'yt- cakes. May he celebrate a "gift of life" ceremony.

Speech of Atum: Words to be spoken by Atum: I have given to you all life and dominion issuing from me.

B. The son of Rē', Tuthmosis, gleaming-of-diadems, 1563
given life like Rē'.

The scene is described thus: Offering wine. May he celebrate a "gift of life" ceremony.

Speech of the god: Words to be spoken by Rē'-Ḥarakhty: I have given to you all health.

502 Small Stela from Memphis

(Petrie *Memphis* I, pl.VIII 4.)

Description:

The king on left smites a prisoner in the presence of a god:

The god: Ptaḥ, lord of heaven, lord of earth.

Inscription on the left hand side of the frame:

Horus, "Mighty bull, son of Atum", king of Upper and Lower Egypt, lord of the Two Lands, Menkheperurē', beloved of Amun, king of the gods.

Inscription on the right hand side of the frame:

Horus, "Mighty bull, perfect of diadems", son of Rē', lord-of-diadems, Tuthmosis, gleaming-of-diadems (beloved) of Ptaḥ, lord of Truth, king of the Two Lands.

503. Inscription on a Bronze Bowl

(Nash *PSBA* 29,175), pl. II, fig. 1.)

The good god, Menkheperurē', son of Rē', Tuthmosis, gleaming of diadems, given life for ever, beloved of Amun-Rē', dwelling in the mortuary temple of 'Akheperurē' in Thebes.

504 Monuments of Tuthmosis IV in Sinai which display his Regnal Year 15

(Both inscriptions are taken from rock tablets.)

A. (Gardiner-Peet *Inscriptions of Sinai* pl.XX, No. 58.)

Regnal year 4, under the Majesty of the king of Upper and Lower Egypt, Menkheperurē', given life.

B. (loc. cit. pl. XIX, No. 60.)

Regnal year 7, under the Majesty of the king of Upper and Lower Egypt, Menkheperurē'. The good god, Menkheperurē', given life.

Son of Rē', Tuthmosis, gleaming-of(diadems).

The king's daughter, Wazet.

505 <u>Monuments of the king's mother Ti'a</u>

A. <u>Dark granite group statue now in Cairo No. 1167, probably from the Fayûm</u>

(Borchardt <u>Statuen IV</u> 87.)

<u>Description:</u> Only the legs of this statue remain and likewise the throne.

<u>Inscription on the right</u> <u>On front elevation of throne</u>:

The king's mother and great royal wife, Ti'a, may she live.

<u>Inscription on the left of same</u>:

The great royal wife, his beloved, beloved of Suchos of Shedet.

B. <u>Black granite group statue now in Cairo No. 42080, from Karnak</u>

(Legrain <u>Statues</u> 1 46/47, pl. 49.)

<u>Description:</u> This statue shows the king on the left and the queen on the right. They are embracing each other.

<u>Inscription on the right on front elevation of throne</u>:

The good god, Menkheperurē', beloved of Amun-Rē', lord of the thrones of the Two Lands, given life.

<u>Inscription on the left of same</u>:

The great royal wife, his beloved, the king's mother, Ti'a, justified.

506 Inscription on the Top of a Small Naos of Tuthmosis IV, now in Cairo 156

(Roeder Naos p.II, No. 70002, coll. with the original.)

Now his Majesty found this stone in the manner of a divine falcon when he was (yet) a royal child. Then Amun commanded him to exercize the kingship of the Two Lands as Horus, "Mighty bull, perfect-of-diadems", lord-of-diadems, Menkheperurē', given like like Rē'.

507 Remains of a Dedicatory Inscription on Blocks in Karnak

(Chevrier Ann. Serv, 51,572.)

.................Tuthmosis, perfect-of-diadems. He made a shrine opposite of costly sandstone surrounded by pillars.................as one who is attentive to his monuments, Tuthmosis, gleaming-of-diadems, given like and stability like Rē' for ever.

508 Remains of a Relief from Karnak with a Scene depicting the Fourth Pylon in Karnak with a Dedicatory Inscription

(Leclant, Revue d'égypt 8,113, fig. 6; Yoyotte Chronique d'Égypte 55,30.)

.............for Amun, lord of the thrones of the Two Lands undertaking monuments of fine gold..........May he celebrate a "gift of life" ceremony like Rē', for ever.

509 Titles of Tuthmosis IV as seen in the Temple at Amada 15

(Gauthier Le Temple d'Amada)

A. Inscription on pillars in the hypostyle hall

Inscriptions on the first pillar on the left:

To the south: The king of Upper and Lower Egypt, who wears the Double Crown, lord of all foreign lands, Menkheperurē', beloved of Nekhbet of El-kab, given like.

To the east: The good god, who builds monuments, the lord of the Two Lands, Menkheperurē', beloved of Khnum dwelling in Elephantine, like Rē' for ever.

To the north: The good god, lord of joy.........all...... lord of Action, Menkheperurē', given life, son of Rē', beloved of the gods, who subdues all foreign lands, Tuthmosis, gleaming-of-diadems for ever.

Inscriptions on the right pillar on the right:

To the north: The son of Rē', of his body, his beloved, Tuthmosis, gleaming of-diadems, beloved of Anukis, mistress of Sehêl, like Rē' for ever.

To the east: The son of Rē' of his body, Tuthmosis, gleaming-of-diadems, beloved of Satis*, mistress of Elephantine, given life.

To the south: The truly good god, a sovereign to be boasted of, son of Rē', of his body, Tuthmosis, gleaming-of-diadems, lord of might, who increases (his) Sed-festivals. May he celebrate very many.

Inscriptionson the second pillar on the left:

To the east: The good god, lord of the Two Lands, Menkheperurē', beloved of Horus, lord of Buhen, given life.

To the south: Golden Horus, "Great of might", Tuthmosis, gleaming-of-diadems, beloved of Month, dwelling in Armant, like Rē' for ever.

To the west: The son of Rē', of his body, lord of joy, Tuthmosis, gleaming-of-diadems............beloved of Rē' (or Amun-Rē'), living for ever.

Inscriptions on the second column on the right: 1567

To the east: Golden Horus, "Great of might, beloved of Horus, lord of Mi'am, living for ever.

To the north: The good god, lord of joy, Menkheperurē', beloved of Isis the god's mother, given life.

To the west: The king of Upper and Lower Egypt, lord of the Two Lands, lord of action, Menkheperure', beloved of Rē'-Ḥarakhty, like Rē' for ever.

To the south: The king of Upper and Lower Egypt, of Southern Egypt and Northern Egypt, ruler of all foreign lands, Menkheperurē', who has appeared like Rē' for ever, son of Rē' of his body, Tuthmosis, gleaming-of-diadems, beloved of Khepery* for ever.

Inscriptions on the third pillar on the left:

To the east: The son of Rē', whom he has crowned, Tuthmosis, gleaming-of-diadems, beloved of Ptaḥ, lord of truth like Rē' for ever.

To the south: The good god, ruler of rulers, Menkheperurē', beloved of Bata* lord of Sako, given life.

To the west: The king of Upper and Lower Egypt, lord of action, Tuthmosis, gleaming-of-diadems, beloved of Khnum lord of Senmut, living for ever.

To the north: ....this monument, which he made for his father Rē', that he may be given all life, stability and dominion..........Tuthmosis, gleaming-of-diadems..............these millions of years.

Inscriptions on the third pillar on the right:

To the east: Golden Horus, great of might, beloved of Bastet, lady of 'Ankh-tawy, living for ever.

To the north: The son of Rē' of his body, Tuthmosis, gleaming of diadems, beloved of Hathor, lady of Gebelein, living for ever.

To the west: Two Ladies, "Stable of kingship", Menkheperurē', beloved of Horus, lord of Kuban, given life.

To the south: ....Menkheperurē', given life........Tuthmosis, gleaming-of-diadems, beloved of..........lord of Heliopolis.

B. Inscriptions upon the architraves 1568

1. (Gauthier p.162, Champollion Not. descr.I 99.)

Words to be spoken by Thoth, lord of the sacred writings, to the great Ennead dwelling in the temple of Rē': Come that you may let us see this great, pure, enduring and splendid monument, this temple of millions of years which the king of Upper and Lower Egypt, Menkheperurē', made for his father Rē'-Atum, the great god who emerges in the horizon. May he celebrate a "gift of life" ceremony like Rē', for ever.

2. (loc. cit.)

(Long) live the good god, the truly valiant one who fends off Kush and reaches her boundaries as if they were such as had never existed; a king brave in might like Month, one stout of heart among the multitude, who traverses foreign lands, Menkheperurē', chosen one of Rē'.

3. (loc. cit.)

King of kings and ruler of rulers, a sovereign to be boasted of, king of Upper and Lower Egypt, Menkheperurē', who has conquered all lands for himself, gleaming-of-diadems, beloved of Amun-Rē', king of the gods, given life, stability, dominion, whilst his heart is joyful together with his ka like (that of) Rē' for ever.

Inscription on the pillars of the hypostyle hall relating to the Sed-festival:

The first occasion of repeating the Sed-festival. May he celebrate very many.

Footnotes to 509

1566.10 A goddess worshipped at Elephantine. She often wears the White Crown flanked by two horns.

1567.6 Khepery. A Heliopolitan form of the emerging deity, Atum, manifest in the sun at dawn. (Rundle-Clark, Myth and Symbol in Ancient Egypt, p.40, foll.)

1567.9 Bull god of Sako in Middle Egypt.

510 <u>Scarabs of Tuthmosis IV</u> 1569

A. (Newberry *Scarabs* pl.30,21)

Menkheperurē', lord of the sweet wind.

B. (pl.30, 22.)

The good god, lord of the Two Lands, Menkheperurē', beloved of Ptaḥ.

C. (pl. 30,24.)

The good god, lord of the Two Lands, Menkheperurē', who appears ravishingly beautiful*.

D. (pl. 30,25.)

The good god, lord of the Two Lands, Menkheperurē', the shining one of all foreign lands.

E. (Petrie *Scarabs* 1163.)

Menkheperurē', rich-in-diadems.

F. Petrie 1164.)

Menkheperurē',appearing in Thebes.

G. (Petrie 1148.)

Menkheperurē', chosen one of Rē'.

H. (Rowe *Scarabs* 543.)

The good god, lord of the Two Lands, Menkheperurē', image of Rē'.

I. (Rowe 536.)

Menkheperurē', beloved of the gods.

K. (Petrie 1151.)

Menkheperurē', image of Amun-Rē'.

Footnote to 510

1569.5 Lit: who appears doubly beautiful.

511 Inscriptions in Tomb No. 95 in Western Thebes belonging to the High Priest of Amun, called Mery. (comp.1414) 1570

Mery inspects cattle and other livestock:

Proceeding to the cattle stalls of the divine offerings of Amun, inspecting the long-horned leaping bulls*, the aviaries and ḥt-'ȝ-fowl from among the offerings of the land of Nubia, long-horned cattle of Retjenu, the game of the desert which the power of his Majesty had taken inasmuch as he is strong...........by the prince and count, confidant of the king when he is in private, the seal being in his hands and on his heart, one whose coming into the royal palace is awaited* in order to carry out this plan of his, superintendent of the prophets of Upper and Lower Egypt, superintendent.................... superintendent of the cows and first prophet of Amun, Mery, justified.

Mery accompanied by his mother presents offerings to the king:

Offering all good and pure things to Amun-Rē', lord of the thrones of the Two Lands, (to) Ḥarakhty and (to) the lord of the Two Lands, 'Akheperurē', by the prince and count, the courtier greatly loved by the king, the righteous beloved, the first prophet of Amun,Mery, justified.

Inspecting the workshops of the temple of Amun and the working procedures of all (kinds of) craftsmanship in silver, gold, lapis lazuli, turquoise, bronze, black copper and raw copper* which his Majesty offered to his father Amun, lord of the thrones of the Two Lands, (pre-eminent in) Karnak, by the prince and count and first prophet of Amun, Mery, justified. 1571

Mery at a feast:

Being seated at a feast and enjoying oneself receiving the gifts which are issued in (his) presence from among the offerings of the lord of gods after having done that which is praiseworthy each day, by the prince and count, the master and governor of Upper Egypt, father of the god belonging to the great throne and first prophet of Amun, Mery, justified with the great god, born of the great nurse of the lord of the Two Lands, Ḥunayt, justified with Osiris.

Titles of Mery as seen on a pillar:

The prince and count, sealbearer of the king of Lower Egypt and superintendent of the two houses of silver belonging to Amun.........

The prince and count, sealbearer of the king of Lower Egypt, and superintendent of the arable lands of Amun.....

The prince and count, sealbearer of the king of Lower Egypt and superintendent of the prophets of Upper and Lower Egypt.

The wife is called:

His "sister", the lady of the house, Mery, justified.

Footnotes to 511

1570.5 sṯp is Helck's restoration. He, however, is also uncertain as to whether this is correct since the traces scarcely resemble □

1570.12 The phrase s3 r is normally an idiom meaning "to revoke." (Lit: back turned to it.) However, this makes little sense in this context. I have taken s3 r i͗yt.f to be an aberrant spelling of the phrase

meaning "one whose coming is awaited," where the scribe has possibly made an error owing to a similarity in sound.

1571.2 ḥr ḫ3st. f lit: upon its desert.

512 <u>Inscriptions in the Tomb of the Royal Tutor or Ḥeḳerneḥeḥ No. 64 in Western Thebes</u> 1572

(Newberry JEA 14, pl.12; coll.)

Description:

Ḥeḳerneḥeḥ and prince Amenḥotp on the right followed by six other princes hand a bouquet to the father of Ḥeḳerneḥeḥ, called Ḥeḳreshu who was tutor to Tuthmosis IV. The latter holds the young prince on his lap.

A. Coming bearing a garland of Amun when he rests in his temple. "May he praise you and may he love you", says the tutor of the royal children when one (i.e. Pharoah) was in.............the escort of the king on his expeditions, the praised one of the good god, tutor of the king's son, Amenḥotp, Ḥeḳerneḥeḥ.

His father is called:

The escort of the king in every place, praised one of him who dwells in the palace, father of the god, educator of the god, one beloved of the sovereign and tutor of the eldest royal son of his body, Ḏḥoutmosi, gleaming-of-diadems, Ḥeḳreshu.

Name and titles of the prince who is upon the lap of Ḥeḳreshu

The eldest royal son of his body, his beloved, whom Amun himself has aggrandized to be lord of that which the sun's disc encircles, the lord of the Two Lands, Menkheperurē'.

The prince's pectoral bore the following inscription: 1573

Menkheperurē', chosen one of Rē'. (Lepsius Denkm. III 69a.)

The prince standing before Ḥeḳerneḥeḥ wears a pectoral inscribed as follows:

Menkheperurē', Tuthmosis, gleaming-of-diadems.

(Champollion Not. descr. 1 571.)

He is also called: the king's son of his body, Amenḥotp.

Two of the accompanying princes are called:

The king's son of his body, Amenemḥēt. The king's son, his beloved, Amenḥotp.

Amenemḥēt wears a pectoral bearing the following inscription: Menkheperurē'.

(Lepsius *Denkm.* Text III 260.)

B. Menkheperurē' makes offering accompanied by young prince Ḥekerneḥeḥ

(Lepsius *Denkm.* Text III 261; coll.)

Placing myrrh and incense on the flame and offering all good and pure things "For your ka, Amun-Rē', lord of the thrones of the Two Lands" during his procession of the west at his festival of the valley, by his attendant in every place, praised one of the good god, whom the lord of
the Two Lands has aggrandized within the palace,/ tutor of 15
the royal children and royal protegé, the beloved of the sovereign...................

C. A man brings a bouquet to Ḥekerneḥeḥ

(Transcribed by Sethe 8,45; coll.)

For your ka, a bouquet of the shrine of Amun when he rests in his temple.............(the ensuing titles are now lost)

Titles of the father Ḥekreshu who brings flowers to the king:

(Champollion *Not. descr.* 1 863 C: Lepsius *Denkm.* Text III 260; coll.)

The prince and count, father of the god and beloved of the god, firm of favour in the palace, LPH, fanbearer at the right of the king, who educated the divine person..... and prophet of the Great of Magic*, Ḥekreshu who brings all (kinds of) fine and pure plants............

Titles of Ḥeḳerneḥeḥ as seen in a ceiling inscription:

(Piehl *Inscr.* 1 141 U; Lepsius *Denkm.* Text III 260; coll.)

The escort of the king on his expeditions, firm in favour in the palace, LPH, the tutor of the king's bodily son, his beloved, Amenḥotp, royal protege, Ḥeḳerneḥeḥ, justified.

Footnote to 512

1574.14 The crown of Upper and Lower Egypt.

513 Statue of Ḏḥoutmosi from the Temple of Mut in Karnak 1575

(Cairo 923, Borchardt, *Statuen* III 156.)

Inscription on the footrest:

An offering which the king gives to Mut, lady of Isheru, lady of heaven and mistress of the gods, that she may grant life, prosperity and health to the ka of the king's son, beloved of the lord of the Two Lands, Ḏḥoutmosi.

An offering which the king gives to Mut, the great, lady of Isheru, who contents the gods, that she may grant happiness, joy, delight, favour and love to the ka of the king's son, Ḏḥoutmosi.

Inscription on the sistrum:

All that which is issued on the altar of the lady of heaven for the ka of the king's son, Ḏḥoutmosi.

Inscription on the handle of the sistrum:

Mut, lady of Isheru.

Inscription on the footrest, on the left:

The king's son, his truly beloved, Ḏḥoutmosi.

On the left of the same:

The tutor of the royal children, Ḥeḳreshu.

514 Graffitto of Ḥeḳerneḥeḥ at Konosso

(Lepsius *Denkm.* Text IV 127; de Morgan *Cat.Mon.*1.69.5)

The first royal herald, Rē', repeating life.

The king's son, 'Akheperurē', repeating life.

The king's son, Amenḥotp.

The royal protegé, Ḥeḳerneḥeḥ, justified.

Graffitto of Ḥeḳreshu at Konosso

(Lepsius *Denkm.* Text IV 128; de Morgan *Cat.Mon.* 1 70,19)

The praised one of Amun-Rē', father of the god, Ḥeḳreshu, justified.

The king's son, Amenḥotp.

The king's son, 'Akheperurē'.

515 Titles of Ḥeḳerneḥeḥ on his Funerary Cones 15

(Daressy, *Recueil de Cones*)

A. The one honoured with Osiris, the tutor of the royal children, Ḥeḳerneḥeḥ. (No. 125.)

B. The Osiris, the royal protegé, Ḥeḳerneḥeḥ, justified. (No. 39.)

C. The Osiris, the superintendent of the horses of his Majesty, Ḥeḳerneḥeḥ, justified. (No. 39.)

D. The Osiris, the royal protegé and royal nurse, Ḥeḳerneḥeḥ, justified. (Berlin No. 8750.)

516 Inscriptions in the Tomb of the Vizier Ḥepu No. 66 in Western Thebes

(Transcribed by Sethe, coll. To be published in Säve-Söderbergh's *Private Tombs at Thebes*)

Ḥepu inspects leather workers:

Inspecting all the handicrafts of the temple of Amun, by the prince and count, father and beloved of the god, spokesman who makes peace in the whole land, eyes of the king in the cities of Upper Egypt and his ears in the nomes of Lower Egypt, who opens his mouth to him concerning whatsoever is truthful and who acts rightfully* for the lord of the Two Lands in the course of every day, the superintendent of the City and vizier, Ḥepu, justified, with the great god.

The titles of Ḥepu as seen in his tomb:

(Transcribed by Sethe, coll.)

The prince and count, father and beloved of the god, superintendent of the lawcourts, spokesman who makes peace in the whole land, who does things of benefit for the lord of the Two Lands, who acts rightfully, the excellent dignitary (begotten) of a dignitary/, the sole companion who 1577
may approach his lord, and his attendant in the Privy Council chamber.............

Inscription on a funerary cone belonging to the Vizier Ḥepu

(Daressy Mém. Miss. VIII, p. 297, No. 270)

The superintendent of the city and vizier, Ḥepu, justified.

Footnote to 516

1576.14 Lit: who presents truth to someone. (See further note to 1541.15.)

517 Inscriptions from the Tomb of the High Steward Thenuna, No. 76 in Western Thebes

(Transcribed by Sethe 10,4; coll.)

Thenuna presents golden vessels to the king:

Presenting..............of fine gold being very many ....I have...........that his Majesty may hear your counsel.........The majordomo was appointed to be chief treasurer...........and he........him in his treasury....................I.......them under the authority*..................

Below this is a vertical column of inscription:

................in every place...........(the rest has been hacked away.)

Thenuna receives gifts: 15

(Piehl Inscr. hiérogl. 1 108; Brugsch Recueil de Monuments égyptiens II LXVI, 2a; coll.)

Coming bearing a bouquet of Amun-Rē', lord of the thrones of the Two Lands, when he rests in his temple. May he praise you, may he love you and may he grant you a lifetime without tribulation and a happy old age with the king, for the ka of the prince and count, well-beloved courtier, the intimate friend of the king whom he loves, great chief spokesman in the whole land, to whom is related that which is in the heart, one who is as inscrutable* as a hidden spring, a true pupil of the king, his beloved, who does that which he who is within the palace praises, the sovereign's unique and devoted one, whom the lord of the Two Lands has aggrandized within his house, he to whom the taxes of the Two Lands and the dues of Upper and Lower Egypt are returned, who fills the palace with sustenance and provisions, who nourishes......with all good things..........true of heart belonging to the good god.............

Thenuuna makes offering: 15

(Piehl. Inscr. hiérogl. I CVIII E a; coll.)

Offering, myrrh, incense and all good and pure things to Amun-Rē', lord of the thrones of the Two Lands, by the prince and count, sealbearer of the king of Lower Egypt, sole friend and intimate companion of the king whom he loves, an official at the head of the common people, the excellent confidant of the lord of the Two Lands, praised one of the good god, who has the entrée to his lord in the hallowed place, who goes out from the palace, LPH, praised, he to whom is related all affairs inasmuch as he is devoted to the king, the attendant of the lord of the Two Lands in every place which he has trodden, he whom the lord of the Two Lands himself instructed for he knows that he would do things of benefit, the eyes of the king of Upper Egypt and ears of the king of Lower Egypt, favourite of Horus in his palace, superintendent of the cows of Amun..........steward of the estate of his Majesty, fanbearer at the right of the king, Thenuna, justified.

Titles of Thenuna: 1580

A. (From a prayer, Piehl. loc.cit. I CVIII, E.β coll.)

Prince and count, intimate friend of the king, his beloved, a unique and excellent one to whom the heart is opened*, who hears the affairs of the secret chamber, pupil of Horus in his palace, a plummet* of the king within the entourage, balance of the common people, the high steward ....

B. (Rec. Trav. 11,158 f; coll.) Inscription on a pillar

..................eyes of the king of Upper Egypt and ears of the king of Lower Egypt............possessor of love............in the palace...........who goes forth praised, the excellent confidant of the lord of the Two Lands, praised one of the good god, the truly attentive administrator, whom the good god loves, the high steward of the king, Thenuna, justified.

C. (Champollion Not. descr. 1 829; coll.) Inscription on a pillar 1581

The prince and count, sealbearer of the king of Lower Egypt, majordomo of the king, master of secrets of the Two Serpent Goddesses*, intimate friend among the courtiers who may approach* the king, who controls the affairs of men, the unique one, confidant of the lord of the Two Lands and praised one of him who is within the palace, he whom the king has aggrandized because of his devotion, who is not remiss concerning that which has been enjoined upon him, the superintendent of the cattle of Amun, and high steward of the king, Thenuna, justified.

D. (Rec. Trav. 11,158 h; coll.) Inscription on a pillar

The prince and count, father and beloved of the god, sealbearer of the king of Lower Egypt, sole friend, magnate of the king of Lower Egypt, great man of the king of Upper Egypt, whom Horus has promoted within the palace..........

His "sister", his beloved, Nebttaui, justified.

<u>Note</u>: According to Champollion (<u>Not descr</u>. 1 481) the tomb contained pictures of gold statuettes of the king and his mother. The inscriptions on these were as follows:-

The good god, Menkheperurē'.

The great royal wife, Ti'a, may she live.

<u>Footnotes to 517</u>

1577.17 Helck would restore this to <u>sn r ḫt</u>

1578.11 <u>ḥ3p ḫt</u> Lit: concealed of body.

1580.4 This should rather read <u>wb3 n.f ỉb</u>

1580.7 i.e. he is able to judge wisely among men. We use a similar metaphor when we speak of a man's having a "balanced judgment".

1581.3 The Crowns

1581.4 This should rather read <u>tkn</u>

518 <u>Inscriptions in the Tomb of the Chief Treasurer Sebekḥotp No. 63 in Western Thebes</u> 15

<u>Sebekḥotp inspects the palace granaries</u>:

(Piehl <u>Inscr. hiérogl</u>. 1 124 N; coll.)

Inspecting the granaries of the palace, LPH, which are richly stocked, and calculating the grain consisting of barley and emmer, by the prince and count, sealbearer of the king of Lower Egypt, sole friend and associate of Nepri* the lord of sustenance*, companion of the lords of the granary* which is filled to overflowing, the heaps reaching unto the sky, the excellent confidant of the lord of the Two Lands, praised one of the good god, who does that which he who is within the palace praises in the course of every day, who fills the palace with silver and gold, the chief treasurer, Sebekḥotp.

Sebekḥotp and his wife receive offerings:

(Lepsius Denkm. Text III 261; coll.)

The prince and count, father of the god, beloved of the god, intimate friend of Horus in his palace, magnate in the king's house and an important man in the palace........... one skilled in counsel who acts rightfully for the lord of truth for he knows that he delights thereat,/ the praised 1583
one of the good god, the mayor of the southern canal* and of the lake of Sebek, superintendent of the prophets of Sebek who belongs to Shedet, and chief treasurer, Sebekḥotp, justified, son of the treasurer, Min, justified.

The names and titles of the mother:

The nurse of the king's daughter of his body, Ti'a who is efficient at suckling, great one of the harim of Sebek who belongs to Shedet, royal favourite,Meryt, called ....

She holds a child upon her lap, who represents the later wife of Amenophis II:

The king's daughter of his body, Ti'a.

The name of a son who is making offering to the couple:

(Lepsius Denkm. Text III 261.)

His son, his beloved, the prophet of Sebek who belongs to Shedet and mayor of the canal of Sebek, Paser.

Behind him stands:

The first prophet of the moon, Ḏḥout.

Inferiors of the chief treasurer who are represented in the tomb:

(Transcribed by Sethe 8, 40; coll.)

The offering bearer of the chief treasurer, Menna.

The district superintendent of the chief treasurer, Ptaḥmosi.

Inscription describing a scene, now destroyed: 158

(Transcribed by Helck)

Inspecting..............in order to stock up with incense..........and in order to offer pellets of incense by all.........of the temple of Amun by the prince and count, who is firm in favour in the palace, and chief treasurer, Sebekḥotp, justified.

Sebekḥotp spears fish:

(Transcribed by Helck)

Crossing the swamps and traversing the bird-pools, amusing oneself spearing fish in the backwaters, by the prince and count, the praised one of the good god, the upright man of Horus in his palace in the course of every day, mayor of the lake of Sebek who belongs to Shedet, chief treasurer, Sebekḥotp, justified.

Titles of Sebekḥotp

(Transcribed by Helck)

The prince and count, the unique and devoted one belonging to the sovereign, praised one of him who is in the palace, fanbearer at the right of the king and chief treasurer, Sebekḥotp, son of the chief treasurer, Min, justified.

His "sister", his dearly beloved.............

Footnotes to 518

1582.8 The corn god.

1582.8 Lit: staff of life plants.

1582.9 This is Helck's tentative reading.

1583.1 The canal herein mentioned is that leading south from Lake Moeris, and the precursor of the modern Bahr Yusuf.

519 Statue of the Chief Treasurer, Sebekḥotp, probably from Memphis, showing him engaged in reading: 1585

(Borchardt Statuen IV p.51, fig. 162.)

Inscription on the footrest:

All that which is issued upon his altar for the ka of the chief treasurer and valiant man of the king, Sebekḥotp, begotten by the chief treasurer, Min.....................

Inscription on the back column:

An offering which the king gives to Ptaḥ............. and to all the gods of Memphis, and to Sekhmet, the beloved of Ptaḥ (that they may grant).............during all their festivals of heaven and earth, for the ka of the chief treasurer Sebekḥotp, justified.

Inscription on the front and on the right-hand side of the base:

The chief treasurer, Sebekḥotp, justified, he says... ....Rē'...........I performed for him remarkable wonders on account of which his Majesty praised him (sic) promoting him among the royal children inasmuch as his character was excellent.

1520 Granite Statue of the Mayor of the Fayûm , Sebekḥotp, now in Berlin No. 11635 1586

(Roeder Berl. Inschr. II, p.45; Brugsch.ZÄS XXXI 1,p.23.)

Note: This is not the same person as the chief treasurer who is his namesake.

Inscription on the base:

An offering which the king gives to Amun-Rē', the great god and lord of the Fayûm, that he may grant all that which is issued upon his offering table in the course of every day during all his festivals of heaven and earth which take place in his shrine, to the ka of the prince and count, the mayor of the lake of Sebek, Sebekḥotp, justified, begotten of the dignitary and mayor of the Fayûm, Kap, justified, born of the lady of the house, Meryt.

Inscription upon the papyrus which Sebekḥotp holds on **his knees:**

An offering which the king gives to Sebek, who belongs to Shedet and to Horus who dwells in Shedet whose Atef crown has tall plumes, the pre-eminent one, the (divine) lord who is abundant in ladies* that he may grant all that which comes forth upon his offering table in the course of every day, entry to and exit from his shrine in the favour of the good god, the receipt of the offerings which his ka gives when the god is in possession of his oblations, to the ka of the prince and count, the attendant of the lord of the Two Lands, in the islands within the Fayûm, the true intimate friend of his lord, superintendent of the marsh-lands, superintendent of cattle, superintendent of the granary, superintendent of works, superintendent of the treasury and superintendent of the prophets of Sebek who belongs to Shedet, the great mayor in the Fayûm, Sebek-ḥotp, repeating life, possessor of honour.

Footnote to 520

1586.12 This is only a tentative translation. "Abundant in ladies" suggests Sebek's sexual potency. The title is almost certainly correctly written because it reoccurs in 1587.3 with identical spelling.

521 A Statue of the same Sebekḥotp now in Marseilles 1587

(Naville Rec. Trav. 1, p.107 ff, with plate after p.139)

Description: Black Granite. Sebekḥotp is shown kneeling and holding a lotus.

Offering inscription:

An offering which the king gives to Sebek, who belongs to Shedet and to Horus who dwells in Shedet, whose Atef crown has tall plumes, the pre-eminent one, the lord who is abundant in ladies*, that he may grant all that which is issued upon his offering table in the course of every day, entry to and exit from his shrine in the favour of the good god, and the receipt of the offerings which his ka gives when the god is in possession of his oblations, to the ka of the prince and count, the attendant of the lord of the Two Lands in the islands within the Fayum, the true favourite of his lord, superintendent of the marshlands (designated) for recreation, superintendent of the prophets of Sebek, who belongs to Shedet and great mayor in the Fayûm, Sebekḥotp, justified.

Inscription on the right:

An offering which the king gives to the ka of the prince and count, Sebekḥotp. He says: I followed his Majesty, whilst being the confidant of the lord of the Two Lands, when his Majesty was taking recreation, enjoying himself on his hunting trip in a canoe crossing the marshes of the Fayum, and traversing the fenlands, bringing down birds with a throwstick/ and spearing fish, the image of a 1588
king beloved of the Fen Goddess, a..........beloved of Sebek, the fowler and fisherman who succeeds by means of his vigour when I was his attendant.

Inscription on the left:

An offering which the king gives to Sebek of Shedet and to Osiris who dwells in the Fayûm, that they may grant invocation offerings of bread and beer, oxen and fowl, clothing, alabaster, incense and oil to the ka of the prince and count, superintendent of the prophets of Sebek, Sebekḥotp. He says: O (you) living upon earth, fathers of the god, w'ab priests, lector priests and all the priesthood, may Sebek of Shedet and Horus who dwells in Shedet praise you as you say: An offering which the king gives, a thousand of all good and pure things for the ka of the mayor of the southern lake and of the northern lake*, Sebekḥotp, begotten by the dignitary and Mayor, Kap, justified, and born of the lady of the house, Meryt, justified.

Footnotes to 521

1587.3 See note to 1586.12.

1588.14 The Fayûm was divided into two administrative districts.

522 <u>Inscriptions from the Tomb of the Scribe of Recruits, Ḥaremḥab No. 78 now in Western Thebes.</u> 158

(Bouriant <u>Mém. Miss V Tomb. de Harmhabi</u> pl.V; Lepsius <u>Denkm</u>. III 78a; coll.)

A. <u>Biographical inscription</u>:

<u>Description</u>:

The scene shows Ma'at on the right and Thoth on the left. In the centre Horus weighs the heart of the deceased.

<u>Inscription</u>:

Giving praise to Osiris, foremost of westerners, kissing the ground before Wennefer, lord of Abydos, the great god and lord of heaven.

I give praise to you, O good god. You are acclaimed daily. I followed in the steps of the good god, lord of the Two Lands, 'Akheperurē', given life, his son, his beloved, the lord of diadems, Menkheperurē', given life, and of his son, his beloved, lord of the foreign lands, Nebma'etrē', son of Rē', Amenophis, ruler of Thebes, beloved of Amun. There was no transgression against anything which they said and none of the people belonging to them said, "Look what is being inflicted on us!" There was no injurious act and no accusation occurred. No falsehood had overtaken me* since my birth; rather I acted rightfully for the lord of all. I was, in fact, a kindly man in the presence of the god, one who had integrity of heart, integrity of word and integrity of deed*.

Let your hearts be glad, O lords of eternity and glorious spirits of the necropolis! See, it is from this land of the living in order to be with you in the hallowed land that I have come. I am one of you. Evil is my abhorrence. It is upon the beautiful road of righteousness that I have come in order that I may make all limbs whole, then my soul shall live, being divine and great with spiritual power. Osiris.............. 159

O, you gods who are in heaven, O,you gods who are upon earth, O, you gods who are within the necropolis, O, all you gods of the crew who row Rē', and who convey the great god to his horizon, may you commend my words to the lords of eternity as the plea of a humble servant to his lord, that he may cause me to rest in (my) habitation of eternity, even in my cavern of everlasting, whilst the Lord of Life rests in its (proper) place, (thus) says.... ....

B. Inscriptions accompanying a scene depicting a feast: 1591

(Bouriant loc. cit. p.426 and pl.II: coll. Sethe)

Speech of Ḥaremḥab's mother to her son:

Your beautiful scent belongs to God's land and you are loved by mankind, O, praised one! Your mother, the lady of the house, Isis, justified and honoured.

Haremḥab holds a princess on his lap:

The king's daughter, Amenemōpet.

The song of two musicians:

For your ka!

Spend a happy day in your beautiful house of eternity, even in your dwelling place of everlasting, with the harp* in your hand.

Bind garlands, anoint (yourself) with finest oil and partake of a happy day, your mind being glad and your heart in ecstasy when you behold Amun! May he cause you to live among men, being praised in the land of the living. Mut comes in the radiance of her beautiful face, that she may grant food; (also) to bear her two sistra and to mix drinks in a bowl of gold enclosed in a similar one of lapis lazuli, filled with................

Officers receive drinks: 1592

For your kas, O (you) troop captains of his Majesty. Spend a happy day in the presence of the royal scribe, his truly beloved.

Another song:

Incense, finest oil, oxen......the prime goods of Amun,
on the Morning of Appearance when he shines forth in Karnak to receive good things,
which are taken in the hand, O Royal scribe who is daily praised,
from your gracious countenance, O, lord of food.
Your fragrance comes from God's land.

C. Egyptians, Syrians and Nubians bring gifts to the king:

(Bouriant loc. cit. pl. IV.)

One Nubian chieftain is called:

The wretched chieftain of wretched Kush.

Two Egyptians, bearing gifts, are called:

The royal steward.

The steward of the private chamber of Pharoah.

D. Ḥaremḥab and his brothers bring gifts to Tuthmosis IV

(Bouriant loc. cit. pl. III, p.42. coll.)

The names and speeches of the brothers: 1593

For your ka, receive all (kinds of) good and pure plants, says...........his brother, his beloved, the troop captain of the skirmishers* of his Majesty, Amenemḥēt and his brother, his beloved, Amenḥotp.

E. Ḥaremḥab makes offering:

(Bouriant loc. cit. p. 427/8 fig. 4; coll. Sethe.)

Receive good things, O Amun-Rē', Ptaḥ, Thoth, Atum and all gods of the west, comprising myrrh, incense, fowl and choice items of food which are doubly pure. May you preserve the ruler and may you grant to him millions of years each day and even for ever.

F. Ḥaremḥab on a bird hunt:

(Bouriant loc. cit. p. 429, pl. VI: coll.)

Enjoying oneself beholding pleasant things and engaging in field sports with the art of the Fen Goddess which is carried out therein with the wild birds of the Delta marshes, by the prince and count, confidant of the king, favourite of Horus in his palace..........Ḥaremḥab, justified.

G. Ḥaremḥab spears fish: 1594

(Bouriant loc. cit. p.429, pl.VI: coll.)

Amusing oneself, beholding pleasant things, going on the hunt and playing the part of the Fen Goddess with every (kind of) skill; traversing the birdpools and crossing the swamps whilst spearing fish in the numerous backwaters, by the prince and count, the excellent confidant of the lord of the Two Lands, the praised one of the good god, attendant of the lord of might in all foreign lands whilst watching him travel on water and upon land*, fanbearer at the right of the king, praised one who has emerged from the body of a praised one, the superintendent of cattle and superintendent of the arable lands of Amun, superintendent of the prophets of Upper and Lower Egypt, Ḥaremḥab, justified.

H. Inscriptions accompanying a scene depicting a meal:

(Bouriant loc. cit. pl.1, p. 428, coll.)

The speech of the wife:

For your ka! Spend a happy day in your beautiful house of eternity, even in your habitation of everlasting/ 1595
your face turned towards Amun-Rē'. Your lord, may he love you*. From your "sister" the lady of the house. (the rest of the line has been left blank.)

A woman standing behind him says:

Receive garlands, smear on finest oil and partake of a happy day in the favour of the good god of Western Thebes;

his "sister" (gap left uninscribed), justified.

Inscription accompanying Ḥaremḥab:

By the prince and count, the excellent confidant of his lord, the praised one who emerged from the body of a praised one, eyes of the king in the whole land, attendant of the lord of the Two Lands in the southern and northern foreign lands, who enters bearing pleasant matters into the place where the king is, who emerged from the palace, LPH, with favour, the royal scribe, Ḥaremḥab, justified ....of the king, who leads him by night as by day.

I. The titles of Ḥaremḥab as seen in his tomb:

(Bouriant loc. cit. pl.V; coll.)

(a) The prince and count, excellent confidant of the lord of the Two Lands, praised one of the good god, fan-bearer to the right of the king, the real royal scribe,
his beloved/, superintendent of the arable lands of Amun, 1596
superintendent of the calves, cows and bulls of Amun, foreman of works of Amun, superintendent of the prophets of Upper and Lower Egypt, superintendent of all the royal scribes of the army, superintendent of horned animals, superintendent of feathered and scaly animals, the royal scribe, scribe of recruits and superintendent of horses ....

(b) (Bouriant loc. cit. p. 429, pl. VI; coll.)

The prince and count, excellent confidant of the lord of the Two Lands, praised one of the good god, eyes of the king in the whole land, intimate friend of Horus in his palace...............attendant of the lord of power in the southern and northern foreign lands, the praised one who emerged from the body of a praised one, the real royal scribe, his beloved, scribe of recruits, Ḥaremḥab, justified.

The name and titles of the wife of Ḥaremḥab:

(Bouriant loc. cit. pl.1; coll.)

His "sister", his dearly beloved, the lady of the house and chantress of Amun in Opet, Ithuy.

Footnotes to 522

1589.17 n ỉw grg ḥ3.ỉ. Lit: no falsehood came behind me.

1589.20 wḏ3 ỉb wḏ3 r wḏ3 ḏrwt. Lit: whole in heart, whole in speech and whole in hand. A difficult phrase to translate without losing the assonance of the original. "Integrity" seems to be the nearest approximation to wḏ3 which has involved altering the construction in translation.

1591.11 Schott, Wüstenthal 126 emends bnt" to snt, wife. See also 1593.2 (Helck Übersetzung p.167, n.2.)

1593.4 mg3 - see Anastasi II 6, 7. Caminos LEM p.53.

1594.10 Helck has emended this to m33.f ḥnd. f. ḥr mw ḥr t3.

1595.1 Helck has emended this to mry.f tw.

523 Graffitti of the Scribe of Recruits Ḥaremḥab at Konosso 1597

A. (Petrie A Season in Egypt 1 35; de Morgan Cat.Mon.1, p.69, No. 12.)

The royal scribe and scribe of recruits, Ḥaremḥab, the escort of his lord on his expeditions in the northern and southern foreign lands, Ḥuy..........ty.

B. (Petrie A Season in Egypt 1 30.)

The superintendent of the granaries of Upper and Lower Egypt, and grain accountant of the lord of the Two Lands, Menuy.

The royal scribe and scribe of recruits, Ḥaremḥab.

The royal scribe, Wepwawetmosi.

524 Inscriptions from the Tomb of a Commander of the Chariotry, No. 1 in Western Thebes

Syrians bring tribute to the king:

(Champollion *Not. descr*. 1 838; transcribed by Sethe 10,57; Wreszinski *Atlas* 1 290, coll.)

Bringing tribute of Naharin by the chieftains of this foreign land in order that they may be given the breath of life, and kissing the ground very many times before the lord of the Two Lands, when they come bearing their tribute to the lord of the Two Lands: Give us the breath which you grant, O, king!

The chieftains of Naharin are come in the mercy of 159
his Majesty bearing tribute upon their backs when they hear...................

The dead man makes an offering:

(Champollion *Not. descr*. 1 840; coll.)

Offering to Amun-Rē', king of the gods and to Rē'-Ḥarakhty..............by the prince and count, the excellent confidant of his lord, praised one of the good god, to whom all affairs are related inasmuch as he is serviceable to the king, the attendant of the lord of the Two Lands in every place which he has trodden, troop captain of the good god and chief of police............

The dead man spears fish:

(Transcribed by Sethe 10,57; coll.)

Enjoying oneself, beholding pleasant things, traversing the bird-pools and spearing fish, by the excellent confidant of his lord, praised one of the good god, attendant of the lord of the Two Lands, who is never absent from the feet of the lord of the Two Lands by night or day, to whom are related all affairs inasmuch as he is serviceable to the king.............

Another inscription: 1599

(Transcribed by Helck)

.................with him, superintendent of the horses, the brave man of the king, and praised one of the good god........(two lines have been obliterated at this point.)

Inscription on the throne of the king:

Giving praise to the lord of the Two Lands by the escort of his Majesty.

525 Inscriptions in the Tomb of the Palace Employee, Ptaḥemhēt No. 77 in Western Thebes

(Lepsius *Denkm.* Text III 272; coll.)

Inspecting all (kinds of) good and pure things on the great quay of the mortuary temple of Menkheperurē' within the temple of Amun which his Majesty made anew for his father Amun-Rē', by the great confidant of the lord of the Two Lands, the praised one of the good god, eyes of the king of Upper Egypt and ears of the king of Lower Egypt and favourite of Horus in his palace, Ptaḥemhēt*.

Inscription accompanying Ptaḥemhēt

...................by the fanbearer of the lord of the Two Lands, Ptaḥemhēt.

Ptaḥemhēt makes offering on a brazier followed by man with bouquet 1600

(Transcribed by Helck)

Offering all good and pure things to Amun-Rē', lord of the thrones of the Two Lands, to Osiris, lord of the hallowed land and to all the gods of the west, by the excellent confidant of his lord, the praised one of the good god, chief of directors with regard to construction works, who does that which his lord praises and who does things of benefit for the lord of the Two Lands in the efficient execution of all his commissions, one who has been rewarded with the treasures which the king gives consisting of gifts from among the booty of the ruler, (from among) the dues of all foreign lands............

Ptaḫemhēt hunts birds:

(Transcribed by Helck)

Crossing the swamps and traversing the bird-pools, enjoying oneself spearing fish in the backwaters, by the beloved of the Fen Goddess and companion of the lady of the fish-catch, the prince and count, confidant of the good god, the praised one who emerged from the body of a praised one, the royal protegé.............

The song of the musicians: 16(

(Transcribed by Helck)

.............your ka.......
Drink until drunkennness, spend a holiday,
your lifetime being happy in the house of
Amun daily
until you reach the city of eternity.
No-one shall forget your name.
All your kindred say, "You are come safely."
Men embrace him
....................pleasant
....................your....
Bringing....................

The brother of Ptaḫemhēt:

His brother, the charioteer, Nebsen.

Beside stand two other people:

The royal protegé, Nezem, justified.

The royal protegé, Paser.

Footnote to 525

1599.17 Emended by Helck to ỉmy-ỉb n Ḥr m pr.f Ptḥ-m-ḥ3t

526 Graffitto of Amenemḥab at Konosso

(Petrie A Season in Egypt 1 41; de Morgan Cat. Mon. 1, p.69, No. 11.)

The royal protegé, Amenemḥab, called Kyky.

527 Inscriptions from Tomb No. 116 in Western Thebes; the owner's name and titles have been obliterated 1602

(Lepsius Denkm. Text III 273; Champollion Not. descr. 1 503; transcribed by Sethe 10, 55; now buried.)

A woman hands a drink to the dead man:

For your ka, O prince and excellent confidant of the lord of the Two Lands, the praised one of this good god, who is not absent from the lord of the Two Lands in any foreign country...................

The speech of the daughter:

Spend a happy day in your beautiful house of eternity, even in your habitation of everlasting, with the lord of life* resting in its (proper) place. By your daughter, your beloved Mi.....

Note: In the tomb the cartouche of Tuthmosis IV has been superimposed upon that of Amenophis II.

Footnote to 527

1602.12 The coffin.

528 Inscriptions in the Tomb of the Scribe Nakht, No. 52 in Western Thebes

(Davies, The Tomb of Nakht at Thebes)

Inscription on the stela belonging to a stelophorous statue 1603

(Davies, loc. cit. p. 38.)

Inscription:

Praising Rē' when he rises until his setting in life occurs, by the skywatcher of Amun, the scribe Nakht, justified.

Hail to you Rē', at your rising, to Atum at your glorious setting. You appear and you shine upon the back* of your mother having appeared as king of the gods that Nut may make jubilation to you and Ma'ēt embrace you at every season. You travel the heaven, your heart joyful, whilst the Lake of the Two Knives*, has become calm, the rebel serpent having been overthrown, his arms bound after the knives have severed his vertebrae.

A funerary cone of Nakht:

(Davies, loc. cit. p.42; Daressy Mém. Miss.8, p.297,No. 271.)

The one honoured with Osiris, the skywatcher of Amun and scribe, Nakht, justified.

His "sister", the chantress of Amun, Taui.

Nakht and his wife, with attendants, pour incense on offer- 160
ings to gods.

(Davies, loc. cit. pls. XI and XII.)

Placing myrrh and incense on the flame for Amun, for Rē'-Ḥarakhty, for Osiris, the great god, for Hathor, mistress of Thebes, and for Anubis who is upon his mountain, by the skywatcher of Amun, Nakht.

His "sister", the chantress of Amun, Taui, justified.

Their son hands them a bouquet:

(Davies, loc. cit. pl. XI.)

..................a bouquet after having done that which is praiseworthy, by her son, Amenemopēt, justified.

Nakht inspects the reaping and winnowing of grain:

(Davies, loc. cit. pl.XVIII.)

Sitting in a booth and inspecting the fields by the

skywatcher of Amun, Nakht, justified, with the great god.

<u>Nakht and his wife pour incense on offerings to gods</u>: 1605

(Davies, loc. cit. pls. XI and XVIII.)

Offerings all good and pure things, bread, beer, oxen, fowl, long-horned cattle, short-horned cattle (which have been) thrown onto the brazier, to Amun, to Rē-Ḥarakhty, to Osiris, the great god, to Ḥatḥor, mistress of the desert and to Anubis who is upon his mountain, by the skywatcher of Amun and scribe, Nakht, justified.

His "sister", his dearly beloved, chantress of Amun and lady of the house, Taui, justified.

<u>Nakht spears fish from his papyrus skiff</u>:

(Davies, loc. cit. pl. XXII.)

Crossing the bird-pools and traversing the swamps, amusing oneself whilst spearing fish, by the skywatcher of Amun, Nakht, justified.

<u>Nakht catches birds from his papyrus skiff</u>:

(Davies, loc. cit. pl. XXII.)

Enjoying oneself beholding pleasant things and engaging in the hunt with the art of the Fen Goddess, by the companion of the lady of the bird-catch/, the skywatcher of Amun.... 1606
...........the scribe, Nakht, justified.

His "sister" the chantress of Amun and lady of the house, Taui, she says: "Enjoy yourself with the art of the Fen Goddess."

The water fowl, which he has taken in his season.

<u>Nakht and his wife seated in a kiosk examine produce</u>:

(Davies, loc. cit. pl.XXII.)

Enjoying oneself and seeing fine things consisting of the produce of the fields of Upper and Lower Egypt, by the skywatcher of Amun and scribe, Nakht, justified.

His "sister", his dearly beloved, the chantress of Amun, Taui.

Inscription accompanying a similar scene below:

Sitting in a hall in order to enjoy oneself and beholding the fine produce of Upper and Lower Egypt, by the skywatcher of Amun, the scribe, Nakht.

His "sister", the chantress of Amun, Taui.

Footnotes to 528

1603.12 The abode of Apep (Book of the Dead, Chap.15 - "You (Rē') traverse heaven, your heart being joyful and the Lake of Desuy is content with it)"

1607.7 There is a pun here on psd, "to shine" and psd, "back" which cannot be rendered into English.

529 Inscriptions from the Tomb of the Artist Neḥem'away No. 165 in Western Thebes

(Davies - Gardiner, Five Theban Tombs pl.39.)

Neḥem'away hunts birds:

Enjoying oneself, beholding pleasant things and 1607
hunting with the art of the Fen Goddess, by the praised one of the lady of the hunt, the goldsmith and sculptor of Amun, Neḥem'away, justified.

His "sister" Tentamentet, called Kay, justified.

Neḥem'away spears fish:

Crossing the swamps and traversing the bird-pools, enjoying oneself spearing fish in the backwaters, by the companion of the lady of the hunt, the goldsmith and sculptor of Amun, Neḥem'away, justified.

His "sister", his dearly beloved, the praised one of Hathor, Tentamentet, called Kay.

530 Inscriptions from the Tomb of the Land Surveyor, Menna, No. 69 in Western Thebes

Menna oversees the measuring out of fields:

(Capart Thèbes p.190, fig. 112, coll.)

Taking recreation with the work of the fields by the great confidant of the lord of the Two Lands, the favourite of Horus in his palace/eyes of the king in every place and 1608
superintendent of the arable lands of Amun, Menna, justified with the great god.

Menna observes work in the fields:

(Capart Thèbes p.190, fig. 112, coll.)

Enjoying oneself, beholding pleasant things in your house of justification, by the excellent confidant of his lord, the praised one of the good god, the scribe and superintendent of the ploughlands of Amun, Menna.

His daughters come up to him:

His daughter, his beloved, the praised one of Hathor, the royal favourite and beloved of their (sic) lord, Amenemwaskhet.

The praised one of Amun, Neḥem'away.

Menna accompanied by his wife and two attendants prays to Osiris who is seated in a kiosk

(Capart Thèbes p.228, fig. 148; coll.)

Giving praise to Osiris and kissing the ground before Wennefer by the scribe and overseer of the ploughlands of Amun, Menna; he says:

It is with truth foremost in my heart and with a heart without wrongdoing that I have come to you. May you cause my body to unite itself with the hallowed land whilst my soul goes to eternity/.......the superintendent 1609
of the arable lands of the lord of the Two Lands and superintendent of the arable lands of Amun, Menna: he says:

I give you praise, I extol you, I affirm your beauty. May I be made to rest in the beautiful west in the favour of your ka.

Behind him stands his wife:

His "sister", the lady of the house and chantress of Amun, Ḥenuttaui, justified with the great god.

Menna is also called:

The scribe of the arable lands belonging to the lord of the Two Lands of Upper and Lower Egypt.

His sons are called:

His son, the scribe of accounts for grain belonging to Amun, Si.

His son, the w'ab priest, Kha'.

531 Stela of the Scribe D̲houtnūfer from his Tomb No.104, in Western Thebes

(Hermann Stelen p.30x; coll. with the original)

A number of lines of inscriptions are missing at the beginning 161

....................festival.............../his ship for ferrying............more than the produce.......... ...in the course of every day, for the ka of the real royal scribe, his beloved, D̲houtnūfer, justified: he says: O you living upon earth who shall exist unto eternity, prophets, scribes, lector priests, w'ab priests and soul priests, scribes wise in knowledge who will enter into this tomb and who will read this stela, may your........ endure for you, may you........before truth............. may you praise your local god, may you behold his beauty and may you bequeath your offices to your children after an enduring old age as you say: an offering which the king gives to Amun-Rē', Ḥarakhty, Osiris, lord of eternity, and Anubis who is pre-eminent in the divine booth that they may grant invocation offerings of bread and beer, oxen and fowl, and all good, pleasant and pure things, plants, wine and milk, which are issued in the presence of the lord of eternity, even before the lord of everlasting and in the presence of Ḥatḥor, mistress of all deserts, to the ka of the royal scribe............called Ḏḥoutnūfer, justified, with the great god, the ruler of eternity. (The remaining lines have been left blank.)

532 Sandstone Boundary Stone of an Estate dedicated to the Service of Tuthmosis IV, the Estate being handed over to the Master Craftsman, Khaut, Cairo 34021 1611

(Lacau Stèles du Nouvel Empire I, p.41, pl. XII)

Inscription upon the upper half:

The good god, Menkheperurē', son of Rē', Ḏḥoutmosi, gleaming-of-diadems, given life for ever, beloved of Amun-Rē', lord of the thrones of the Two Lands.

Inscription upon the lower half:

The south-eastern boundary belonging to the soul service of the statue of the king of Upper and Lower Egypt, lord of the Two Lands, Menkheperurē', given life, given as a favour of the king to the w'ab priest and master craftsman of Amun, Khaut, on low-lying arable land of five arouras and the new land of Tantshen'au (which are) for the divine offerings.

533 Stela of a Master Builder, Neferḥēt, now in Cairo, No. 34022

(Lacau Stèles du Nouvel Empire 1, p.42, pl. XIII.)

Description. Material; limestone. The scene in the upper register shows the king on the left worshipping a goddess, who is seated on the right. Beneath the disc of the sun is the name, Menkheperurē'.

Accompanying inscriptions:

The king: The son of Rē', of his body, Tuthmosis, gleaming-of-diadems like Rē', for ever.

The goddess: Nut, who gave birth to the gods, who dwells in Abydos.

Principal inscription: 161

(Long) live Horus, "Mighty bull, perfect-of-diadems", Two Ladies, "Stable of kingship like Atum", Golden Horus, "The great of strength who fends off the Nine Bows", the good god, image of Rē' and son of Amun, who tramples foreign lands, who carries off the inhabitants of the south as living prisoners whilst the inhabitants of the north (fall) subject to his sword as his father has decreed for him, the son of Isis. (He is) a son more dear to his heart than all (other) kings who have ever been, the king of Upper and Lower Egypt, lord of the Two Lands, lord of action, Menkheperurē', the son of Rē' of his body, his beloved, lord of all foreign lands, Tuthmosis, gleaming-of-diadems, beloved of Nut, given life for ever.

Second inscription: (now destroyed.)

The escort of the king in his every place, praised one of the good god, Neferḥēt. Giving praise to Nut and kissing the ground before the lady of heaven by the superintendent of works of the mortuary temple of Pharoah, LPH, in Abydos, Neferḥēt.

534 Titles of the same Master Builder, Neferḥēt, as seen on a Stela now in the British Museum, No. 148

(Hierogl. Texts VII 43.)

a. The superintendent of works of the mortuary temple in Abydos, Neferḥēt. 161

b. The superintendent of works of the mortuary temple of Pharoah and royal protegé of the lord of the Two Lands, Neferḥēt, justified with the great god.

c. The superintendent of works of the mortuary temple of Menkheperurē', given life, Neferḥēt.

d. The superintendent of works in the mortuary temple of Pharoah in Abydos, Neferḥēt.

535 Two Stelae of the Fanbearer Thuna

A. Stela in Stockholm No. 24

(Mogensen Stèles Égyptiennes au Musée national de Stockholm pp. 23/4; Piehl Inscr. 1 14 A.)

Description:

At the head of the stela is a device showing from left to right: papyrus - wedjat-eye - Anubis recumbent, Anubis recumbent - wedjat-eye, lotus.

Below are opposing images of Neferḥēt adoring Osiris and Isis (left) and Min (right.)

Above the disc of the sun is the name Menkheperurē.

i. Giving praise to Wepwawet (by) the prince and count, sealbearer of the king of Lower Egypt, sole companion and fanbearer at the right of the king, Thuna, justified.

ii. Giving praise to Osiris, kissing the ground before the lord of eternity by the prince and count, sealbearer of the king of Lower Egypt, sole friend and intimate favourite of Horus in his palace, Thuna.

B. Stela in Cairo No. 34023

(Lacau Stèles du Nouvel Empire I, p.44, pl. XIV

Description: Material: limestone. At the head of the stela is a device showing from left to right: wedjat-eye, shen sign over sign for water, wedjat-eye.

Register one shows Osiris seated at an offering table with king Menkheperurē', the deceased and his wife.

Register two shows the deceased and his mother receiving offerings. Not all the texts on the stela are included here.

i. His wife: His wife, the lady of the house, Nubmutes*

ii. His mother: His mother, Ta'at.

Footnote to 535

1613.17 nb mwt.s "her mother's gold" is only tentative. Helck has restored Nwb-m-wsḫt but he, too, is uncertain of this.

536 Black Granite Statue of the High Steward of the King, Meryrē'. 161.

(Once in Mitau, Wreszinski ZÄS 67, 132, pl.9.)

Inscription on stela which the deceased is holding:

Praising Rē' when he rises by the prince and count, sealbearer of the king of Lower Egypt, sole friend, master of ceremonies of Amun and high steward of the king Meryrē'; he says, "Hail to you Rē', lord of eternity who made the heavens, the unique and only god, lord of the universe and father of the gods. I give praise unto you that I may extol you, that I may revere the beauty of your Majesty. May you establish my favour in the presence of the king and the love of me before the lord of the Two Lands.

Inscription on base:

May you let me be buried in the beautiful west within my habitation of eternity as you did for me upon earth. The superintendent of the two houses of gold and the two houses of silver, and high steward, Meryrē'.

537 Funerary Cone of the same Meryrē'

(Bull Inst. franç. VI 15)

The high steward of the king, Meryrē'.

538 Palette of the High Steward Meryrē' in the British Museum, No. 5512 16

(Glanville JEA 18, 57, pl VII 3.)

Horizontal inscription above ink wells:

(Long) live the good god, lord of the Two Lands, Menkherperurē', beloved of Thoth who is pre-eminent in Ḥesret.

Inscription on the left of pen groove:

An offering which the king gives to Amun-Rē', lord of the thrones of the Two Lands, the sole god who lives in truth, that he may grant the pleasant wind which comes forth (from) his nose and his great favour in the palace to the ka of the high steward, Meryrē'.

Inscription on the right of pen groove:

An offering which the king gives to Thoth, lord of the sacred writings that he may grant the knowledge of the writings which came forth from him and understanding of the god's word, to the ka of the prince and count, the nobleman who is at the head of the nobles of the king and high steward of the king, Meryrē'.

Horizontal inscription:

The scribe of the high steward of the king, Thenuna.

539 Stela of Amenḥotp who spent his early career as Officer of Chariotry and his later career as High Priest of Onuris. Brit. Mus. No. 902

(*Hierogl. Texts* VIII, pl.9, Sharpe, *Egypt. Inscr*.1 93.)

Description: Material: limestone 1616

The scene in the upper register shows Amenḥotp adoring Osiris and Wepwawet

Inscription A. accompanies the image of Osiris.
Inscription B. accompanies the image of Wepwawet.
Inscription C. accompanies a scene of the sons of Amenḥotp making offering to their father.

A. Osiris, foremost of westerners and lord of Abydos. Giving praise to Osiris and kissing the ground before Wennefer (by) the first prophet of Onuris, Amenḥotp.

B. Wepwawet, lord of the hallowed land. Giving praise to Wepwawet and kissing the ground before the lord of the hallowed land (by) the first prophet of Onuris, Amenḥotp.

C. His son, the charioteer of his Majesty Ḥaty. A very pure offering which the king gives, it being most pure, for the ka of the first prophet of Onuris, Amenḥotp, justified.

The lady of the house and chantress of Onuris, Ḥenut.

His son, the charioteer of his Majesty, Ḳenna, justified. An offering which the king gives, it being most pure, for the ka of the first prophet of Onuris, Amenḥotp.

His mother, Ry, justified.

<u>Principal inscription</u>:

An offering which the king gives to Osiris, foremost of 1
westerners, to Wepwawet, lord of the hallowed land and to Wennefer in all his names, his images and his true forms, that they may grant transfiguration in heaven with Rē', strength upon earth with Geb and justification in the necropolis with Osiris; (also) to inhale air (laden) with myrrh and incense, cool water, wine, milk, as many funerary meals as possible* and gifts consisting of all (kinds of) fruit, the receipt of the offerings which are issued upon the offering table of the lords of the temple, entry to and exit from the hallowed land whilst receiving the foodstuffs provided, emergence as a living soul, without being turned back from any door of the netherworld, to accompany the god on his travels in the same manner as when upon earth, the receipt of offerings in the presence of the Sole Lord and the pure bread which is issued in the temple, to the ka of the escort of the king on all his expeditions in the foreign lands of the south and north, who came from Naharin to Kurja in his Majesty's train when he was on the battlefield, the attendant of the lord of the Two Lands, stablemaster of his Majesty and first prophet of Onuris, Amenḥotp, justified.

<u>Footnote to 539</u>

1617.8 <u>mỉ 'šꜣ.f</u> An idiom. The literal meaning is "a funeral meal as it is plentiful."

540 <u>Inscriptions from the Tomb of the Chief of Police of</u> 1
<u>Western Thebes, Nebamūn No. 90 in Western Thebes</u>

The appointment to Nebamūn to office:

(Davies, *Tombs of Two Officials*, pl. XXVI

A. Regnal year 6. The conferment of a boon in the Majesty of the palace, LPH, on this day to the prince and commander of the fleet of Upper and Lower Egypt. The command ran (thus): My Majesty commanded acceptance of a gracious retirement in royal favour in order to effect the settlement of the affairs of the standard bearer, Nebamun of the royal ship "Beloved of Amun".

He had reached old age following Pharoah, LPH, in the integrity of his heart, being more efficient today than yesterday doing that which had been enjoined upon him. He was not accused and there was no-one discovered a transgression of which he could be arraigned as a wrong-doer.

Then my Majesty, LPH, commanded that he be installed*
as chief of police in the west of the city in the locality
of Tjembu and in the locality of 'A-bau/ until he reaches 1619
the blessed state, together with providing his household, his cattle, his arable lands, his servants and all his property on water and on land without allowing any interference therein by any inspector of the king - the standard bearer of the ship "Beloved of Amun" and veteran of the army, Nebamūn, justified.

B. Inscription accompanying the scene which concerns the handing over of his official papers and standard:

It is on this account that the royal scribe, Iuny, repeating life, comes.

Note: For the monuments of Iuny, see below.

C. Nebamūn adores Tuthmosis IV:

(loc. cit. pl. XXVI.)

Giving praise to the good god, Menkheperurē'. "I give praise to you, Tuthmosis, gleaming of diadems, the beloved sun", says the prince and count, the excellent confidant of his lord, attendant of the lord of the Two Lands in the foreign lands of south and north and standard bearer, Nebamūn, justified.

D. In front of Nebamūn is a standard surmounted by the image of a ship with the cartouche of Menkheperure' upon the cabin below a flabellum. In another place the ship to which the standard belongs is called: The royal ship, "Beloved of Amun."

(loc. cit. pl. 28.)

Behind the scene of the conferment of office are some 16
members of the police force. These are led by:

(a) The chief of police in Thebes, Teri.
(b) The police deputy, Mana.

E. Nebamun presents Syrian tribute to Tuthmosis IV

(loc. cit. pl. XVIII)

For your ka, O you good god from among the tribute of ....most valiant, the children of the chieftain of Naharin, by the attendant of the lord of the Two Lands in the southern and northern foreign lands and standard bearer of (the ship) "Beloved of Amun", Nebamūn.

Inscription above Syrians who are doing homage:

Giving praise to his Majesty...........

F. Nebamūn escorts the king by ship to Thebes:

(loc. cit. pl. XXIV)

(To) starboard*. Travel westward! O sweet water, bring him who is sailing upstream to the temple of Amun in order to do that which Amun praises.

G. Nebamūn receives news concerning the state of the 162
necropolis:

(loc. cit. pl. XXI

Nebamun is called:

The chief of police of Western Thebes, Nebamūn........

The news is brought to him by:

His brother, the chief of police in Western Thebes, Teri.

The latter says as follows:

The southern district and the northern district are in order.

Speech of two policemen:

What the bearers say: The place is unscathed and in excellent order.

H. Song of marching recruits with their superintendent:

(loc. cit. pl.XXXI.)

He nurtures the young troops, he nurtures the young troops, Amun's ruler, his heart being joyful.

I. Nebamūn accompanied by members of family and a musician make offering to Amun and to Rē'-Ḥarakhty:

(loc. cit. pl. XX.)

Offering all good and pure things in the way of myrrh, incense, legs of meat and fowl to Amun, lord of the thrones of the Two Lands, and to Rē'-Ḥarakhty that they may preserve* the ruler each day, by the prince and count, the excellent confidant of his lord, praised one of the good god, attendant of the lord of the Two Lands in the southern and northern foreign lands and standard bearer of (the ship) "Beloved of Amun", Nebamūn.

His "sister" and dearly beloved, the lady of the house, 1622
Teye.

Song of the lute player:

For your ka, Amun-Rē'.

.............all good and pure things consisting of myrrh and incense, of oxen and short-horned cattle, received at the hand of Nebamūn who praises him each day. I offer to you that he may be among the praised ones in the land of the living.

J. Nebamūn and his wife seated at a feast with two daughters:

(loc. cit. pl. 21.)

Enjoying oneself and spending a holiday in his beautiful house of eternity by him who is firm of favour, a magnate in the palace, who is more efficient today than (he was) yesterday. It is in the following of the king that he has attained an illustrious old age, the standard bearer of (the ship), "Beloved of Amun", a valiant man at the head of the numerous army, Nebamūn, justified.

His "sister", his beloved, of trustworthy character and kindly disposition, who is alike in nature* to her "brother", the lady of the house, Teye, justified.

Their daughter sits next to them: 162

She is called. The royal favourite, his beloved, praised one of the good god, Segerttaui,repeating life.

A girl hands her an object not clearly identifiable with the following words:

For your ka! Spend a holiday O praised one of the good god. From the beloved sister, Weret.

In another place the same daughter is called:

His daughter, his dearly beloved, the royal favourite, praised one of the good god, possessor of favour in the palace, one well-beloved in the presence of the king, Segerttaui.

(loc. cit. pl.22.)

K. Nebamūn and a second wife at a feast, seated with daughter:

(loc. cit. pl.23.)

By the prince and count, great confidant of the lord of the Two Lands, praised one of the good god, standard bearer of (the ship), "Beloved of Amun", Nebamūn.

His "sister", his beloved, the lady of the house, Senisenbut, justified.

Two daughters hand drinking bowls to him: 16

For your ka! in life and in health, O praised one of Amun, in your beautiful house of eternity, even in your habitation of everlasting. Amun gives his favour to you every day. From your daughter, your dearly beloved, Nebttaui, justified, and his daughter, his dearly beloved, Weret, justified.

Song of the musicians:

..........our sistra to her beloved face
which are beautiful in the sight of Nebamūn
when he comes from his offerings, his beart
being joyful.

L. Nebamūn seated on a stool inspects the pressing of grapes:

(Davies loc. cit. pls. 30 and 33.)

Having the grape-harest pressed by the troop captain in Western Thebes and standard bearer, Nebamūn.

M. Nebamūn seated on a stool with two attendants inspects the registration of cattle:

(loc. cit. pl. 33.)

The standard bearer, Nebamūn, justified, has spoken to the scribe, Ḏḥoutnufer: Do not neglect the cattle of Amun, my lord.

N. Nebamūn on left makes offering in front of a temple 1625

(Davies loc. cit. pl. 33.)

Inscriptions upon the door:

The good god, lord of the Two Lands, Nebma'etrē', beloved of Amun Rē', lord of heaven, given life, the son of Rē', his beloved, Amenophis, beloved of Amun-Rē', lord of heaven, given life.

Principal inscription accompanying above scene:

Offering all good and pure things, a thousand of long-horned and short-horned* cattle, fowl, lotus flowers, reeds, lotus buds and all (kinds of) scented plants with sweet perfume to Amun-Rē', "May you preserve the ruler, LPH", says the standard bearer Nebamūn, repeating life......

O. A man dips in jar of grape juice as an offering to Renenutet:

(loc. cit. pl.30.)

For your ka, Renenutet! Give food and sustenance!

P. Inscription on the stela on the north wall:

(Davies loc. cit. pl. 36; Hermann *Stelen* p.25*)

An offering which the king gives to Amun-Rē', lord of the thrones of the Two Lands to Rē'-Ḥarakhty, to Osiris, foremost of westerners, to Ptaḥ-Sokar, lord of Shetyt and to Anubis, who is before the divine booth that they may grant, a thousand invocation offerings of bread and beer, a thousand of oxen and fowl, a thousand of clothing and alabaster, a thousand of incense, a thousand of oil, a thousand of all good and pure things, a thousand of all 162
good and sweet things which the sky gives and the earth creates and which the Nile brings forth from his cavern, (also) to inhale the sweet breath of the north wind, to eat bread, to partake of plants.............consisting of all (kinds of) good things, the receipt of gifts consisting of the fine things among the offerings of the field of reeds, to assume any form which he desires in the following of Wennefer............entry to and exit from the necropolis, without the soul's being held back from that which it desires, emergence as a living soul, to drink water at the river eddy, to breathe in the wind which comes forth from the horizon and the pleasant breeze of the north wind which comes at once; (also) that men may pronounce his name, the arm being bent with offerings, emergence at the (sound of) the voice as soon as he is summoned, the receipt of water at the hands of a soul-priest; (also) that he may have power over water, that he may have power over beer on the offering table that his ka desires, that he may eat bread on the altar
of the lord of all/ and on the offering table of the 162
lords of eternity, that he may cross over in the ferry boat of the necropolis to the islands of the Field of Reeds, that he may pass along the ways without his being turned away at the gates of the netherworld, (but rather) being inundated there with wine and milk, and the receipt of *mdt*-oil, anointing oil, eye-paint, clothing and linen to the ka of the standard bearer of (the ship) "Beloved of Amun", Nebamūn, justified.

There is no unpleasantness with regard to anything, which is said* and the people belonging thereto did not say, "See what is being inflicted on us". There was no injurious act, and no accusation of mine arose. No falsehood of mine had overtaken* me since my birth but rather I acted rightfully for the lord of all. I was, in fact, a kindly man in the presence of the god, one who had integrity of heart, integrity of mind and integrity of deed*.

Let your hearts be glad, O lords of eternity and glorious spirits of the necropolis. See, it is from this land of the living in order to be with you in the hallowed land that I have come/. I am one of you. Evil 1628
is my abhorrence. It is upon the beautiful reed of righteousness that I have come in order to make limbs whole, then the soul shall live, being divine with spiritual power; the Osiris, Nebamūn.

"O you gods who are in heaven and upon earth, O you gods who are in the netherworld, O you divine crew who row Re', and who convey the great god to his horizon in the western part of heaven, may you commend my words to the lord of eternity as the plea of a servant to his lord, that he may cause me to rest in (my) habitation of eternity, even in (my) cavern of everlasting", says the prince and count, the excellent confidant of the lord of the Two Lands, the praised one, eyes of the king of Upper Egypt and ears of the king of Lower Egypt..................Naharin...... .....in the foreign land of Kurja..................

Footnotes to 540

1618.9 Lit. old age.

1618.18 Helck has emended rdỉ.n.f to rdỉ. f

1620.16 Ḥelck has emended ỉmi wrt to read ỉmy-wrt. Ubersetzung p.180, n.6.

1621.16 Ḥelck has emended snbt.sn to read ssnb.sn. Ubersetzung p.181, n.2.

1622.19 An idiom deriving from m3ḫ3t, "balance".

1625.7 This is probably ỉw3 and wndw but the original signs are by no means clear.

Footnotes to 540 contd.

1627.9 — sn cannot mean "they" here because there is no antecedent to which it can refer. It must therefore be the New Kingdom of the third person plural, "anything which is said."

1627.13 — n ỉw grg ḥ3 (ỉ) Lit. no falsehood has come behind me.

1627.16 — See note to 1589.20.

541 Stela of the chief of Police, Nebamūn in the Louvre, C.60 162

(Piehl. Inscr. Hiérogl. 1 13 B.)

An offering which the king gives to the Foremost of Westerners, the great god, lord of Abydos, lord of the cavern mouth, Imiut, lord of the hallowed land, to Ptaḥ-Sokar (of) Shetyt who dwells in the mount of remembrance, to Wepwawet of Upper Egypt and to Wepwawet of Lower Egypt, that they may grant invocation offerings of bread and beer, oxen and fowl, all good and pure things, all pleasant and sweet things, incense, wine, myrrh, food from among the divine offerings, the receipt of the offerings which come forth in their presence and the choicest things which are issued on her (sic) altar, existence there as a dignitary of excellence in the favour of the lords of eternity; (also) that my soul may follow the great god, that the remembrance of me may endure in his temple, that men may come forth to me bearing ds-jars of beer from among the offerings of the lords of eternity, that I may receive meals from a great one when he makes invocation at the altar of the great god and that I may plough...........to the ka of the standard bearer of (the ship) "Beloved of Amun", Nebamūn.

542 A Funerary Cone of Nebamūn:

(Mém. Miss, 8, p.287, No. 166; Ann. Serv. 6, 93.)

The Osiris, the standard bearer of (the ship), "Beloved of Amun", superintendent of the desert of Western Thebes, Nebamūn, justified, with the great god.

543 A Funerary Cone of the brother of Nebamūn, called Turo:

(Mém. Miss 8, p.277, No. 59.)

The one honoured with Osiris, the chief of police, Turo, justified.

544 Limestone Stela of the Master Shipwright, Iunna, now in the British Museum, No. 1332.) 1630

(Hierogl. Texts VIII, pl. 33; Glanville ZÄS AZ 68, 38 ff. pl.2.)

Description: Material: limestone.

The device at the head of the stela shows no unusual features. There are no cartouches whereby the stela can be dated.

The scene below shows Iunna (on right) honouring the barque of Osiris. Inscription C. accompanies the figure of Iunna.

Inscription D. accompanies Iunna and his wife on the left and parents on the right seated at offering tables.

A. Giving praise to Osiris and kissing the ground before Wennefer by Iunna.

B. The master shipwright of the Neshmet barque, the lady of eternity, Iunna, he says: may my local god be behind me and his ka before me. May I follow my lord and become justified.

C. The master craftsman of the Neshmet barque at his (i.e. Osiris') yearly procession on the day of the appearance of the Neshmet barque, Iunna.

D. The master craftsman for the construction of the barques of all the gods of Upper and Lower Egypt and royal protegé, Iunna.

His father is called: His father, the master craftsman of the king, Ḥumasha.

His mother is called: The lady of the house, Nebtes.

E. <u>Principal inscription</u>: 163

The master craftsman of the barque of Amun, (called) Userhēt and royal protegé, Iunna.

The master craftsman of the Neshmet barque, the lady of eternity in Thinis, the royal protegé whom the king loves, Iunna.

The master craftsman of the barque of Atum, the Heliopolitan, and royal protegé, Iunna, repeating life.

The master craftsman of the barque of Ptaḥ in Memphis, the praised one of the good god and royal protegé, Iunna, justified.

The master craftsman of the barque of Sepa* in Heliopolis, the royal protegé, beloved of his lord, the royal protegé, Iunna.

The master craftsman of Ius'as* and Nebtḥotpt in Heliopolis, the royal protegé and praised one of his god, Iunna.

The master craftsman of the barque of the lord of Hermopolis* and of the barque of Khonsu in Thebes, the royal protegé, Iunna.

The master craftsman of the barque of Khnum, lord of Antinoë in Neferusy, the royal protegé, beloved of the lord of the Two Lands, Iunna, the reborn*.

The master craftsman of the barque of Month, lord of Thebes and of the barque of Month, lord of Armant, and royal protegé, Iunna.

The master craftsman of the barque of Amun in the inundation district* and of the barque of Sekhmet in the lake of Pharoah and royal protegé, Iunna. 1632

The master craftsman of the barque of Sebek (of) Shedet and of Horus dwelling in Shedet in the great city, and royal protegé, Iunna.

As to everyone who shall read these words, may these gods whose barques I have built praise you and may they grant to you a happy life, a happy old age and a goodly burial.

Footnotes to 544

1631.10 The centipede god. See Faulkner *Coffin Texts* Spells 91, 227, 280 in which the legs of the deceased are likened to those of Sepa, 414 and 1121.

1631.12 "As she comes, she grows" and Nebtḥotpt, two goddesses of Heliopolis. See Gard. *AEO* 11 146. Mentioned in the Pyramid Texts, line 1210 (b). See Sethe, *Übersetzung und Kommentar*, Vol. V, p.109, where Sethe believes Nebtḥotpt to be a place name personified as a goddess.

1631.14 Thoth.

1631.17 A sportive writing of wḥm 'nḫ. See Gard. *EG* p.475.

1632.1 Helck states that this area apparently lay to the west of Memphis, probably near Gizeh. *Übersetzung* p.186, n.6.

545 Titles of the Captain of the Administration of the Mortuary Temple of Tuthmosis IV, Ipy from his Theban Tomb which is now lost

(Champollion *Not. descr.* 1 518/9; Lepsius *Denkm.* Text III 264.)

A. Superintendent of the ships of Amun belonging to the mortuary temple of the lord of the Two Lands, Menkheperurē', given life, Ipy.

B. The Osiris, superintendent of the ships of the mortuary temple of Menkheperurē' in the temple estate of Amun, Ipy*.

C. The superintendent of the ships in the temple estate of Amun, Ipy.

D. The superintendent of the ships of Menkheperurē' in the temple estate of Amun, Ipy.

Titles of the sons: 1633

His son, the first prophet of Month, Denreg.

His son, who causes his name to live, the count, superintendent of prophets and first prophet and steward of Month, lord of Armant, Denreg, justified.

His son, the first prophet of Menkheperurē', Piay.

His wife was called as follows: His "sister", his beloved, the lady of the house, Meretseger, (after Lepsius.) praised one of Mut, lady of heaven, the lady of the house, Meretseger. (after Champollion.)

Note:

According to Champollion there was a stela that began with the words: An offering which the king gives to Hathor, mistress of Thebes that she ("they" in the text) may grant to me a happy lifetime in the necropolis in the following of king Menkheperurē', given life*.

Footnotes to 545

1632.15 According to Helck this line has been abbreviated and the sign within the enclosure and the enclosure itself are to be interpreted as translated. He has interpreted lines 16 and 17 in the same way.

1633.10 Helck believes that Champollion inadvertently omitted the name of a second god when he transcribed the text, hence di has a plural subject.

546 Inscription on a Stelophorous Statue No. 1238 (1387) in the British Museum.

An offering which the king gives to Amun-Rē', king of the gods, that he may grant life, prosperity and health to the ka of the superintendent of cattle, steward of Amun and scribe of the estate of Menkheperurē', Kaemweset.

The ram of Amun is called: Amun-Rē' of gold.

Note: (On the right shoulder of the figure is a mn sign)

Footnote to 546

1633.17 The word mn probably expresses the wish that the statue may endure.

547 Rock Stela of the Commandant of Sile, Neby, in Sinai 1634

(Gardiner-Peet-Czerny, Inscriptions of Sinai Pl.20, No. 58)

Description:

The scene at the head of the stela below the cornice on right shows the king followed by an official making offering of milk to a goddess.

The king is called:

The good god, Menkheperurē', son of Rē', Ḏhoutmosi, gleaming-of-diadems, given life for ever, belovēd of Ḥatḥor, lady of the turquoise, given life for ever.

He is followed by:

The royal messenger in all foreign lands, the steward of the harîm of the queen, mayor of Sile and royal protegé, Neby.

The date:

Regnal year 4 under the Majesty of the king of Upper and Lower Egypt, Menkheperurē', given life.

548 Stela of the Commandant of Sile, Neby, in Leiden V.43

(Boeser Beschrijvung Steles, p. 13.)

The first register shows Neby praising Osiris:

Giving praise to (Osiris) and kissing the ground before Wennefer by the chief of police and troop captain of Sile, Neby.

His "sister", the lady of the house, his dearly beloved, Tauswert.

The second register shows two offering scenes:

The following receive offerings: The troop captain and mayor of Sile, Neby.

The lady of the house, Tauswert.

They receive offerings from:

His son, Ḥaremḥab.

The following are also recorded:

The w'ab priest of Amun, Amenemḥēt.

The lady of the house, Tathuia.

They receive offerings from:

His daughter, Meretḥor.

Principal inscription: 1635

An offering which the king gives to Osiris, foremost of westerners, the great god and ruler of eternity that he may grant invocation offerings of bread and beer, clothing, alabaster, incense, oil, cool water, wine and milk; (also) to inhale the sweet breath of the north wind, to drink of water at the river-eddy, and all good and pure things to the ka of the prince and count, an important man in his office and magnate in the palace, chief of police, superintendent of the fortresses of the land of Wawat, the troop captain of Sile, superintendent of the fortress, superintendent of the canal and mayor of Sile, Neby.

549 Kneeling Stelophorous Statue of the Viceroy Amenḥotp from Deir el-Medineh

(Alliot *BIFAO* 32, 71; see also Habib Habachi, *Lexicon der Ägyptologie* II 637, Note 58 in which he attributes this stela to Amenḥotp, viceroy in the reign of Tutankhamun)

Praising Rē', when he rises and beholding the sun's disc in the course of the day, without being turned away from anything which is in his keeping, by the viceroy's son of Kush, the royal scribe, superintendent of the cattle of Amun, fanbearer at the right of the king, praised one of the good god, beloved crowned prince* of the lord of the Two Lands, Amenḥotp, justified.

Footnote to 549

1635.20 Helck states that iry p't here was probably used in the same sense as it was used under the Ramessides when it was given to the crowned prince as king's representative. The viceroy of Kush was, after all, the king's representive there.

550 Stela of the Viceroy Amenḥotp in the Ashmolean Museum, Oxford 1636

(PSBA 16, 4, coll.)

Above is the name of the king: Menkheperurē'.

Inscription above an obliterated figure:

Offering all (kinds of) good things by the viceroy and royal scribe, Amenḥotp.

He stands before a goddess who is called:

Isis, the great, the god's mother, mistress of all the gods and lady of heaven.

Principal inscription:

An offering which the king gives to Horus, lord of Buhen and to Isis, the great, the god's mother and mistress of the lands of the south, that they may grant existence on earth in the favour of the king, (also) to spend a happy lifetime, to the ka of the confidant of the king on earth, superintendent of the cattle of Amun, the confidant of Kush in respect of her produce*, seal-bearer to the king of Lower Egypt, magnate in the palace and royal scribe, Amenḥotp.

Footnote to 550

1636.14 r di͗di͗.s. Lit: that which she gives

551 Graffitto of the Viceroy of Kush, Amenḥotp on Sehêl 163

(de Morgan *Cat. Mon.* 1, p.92, No. 108)

The superintendent of the cattle of Amun, foreman of works in Upper and Lower Egypt, stablemaster of his Majesty, viceroy, king's son of Kush, superintendent of the southern foreign lands, valiant man of the king, praised one of the good god and royal scribe, Amenḥotp.

552 Boundary Stela from Wadi Halfa, now in the Ashmolean Museum, Oxford

(*PSBA* 16, 18, coll.)

Description:

The device at the head of the stela shows no unusual features. The scene below shows the king offering to a god.

The king: The good god, lord of action, Menkheperurē'.

The god: Horus, lord of Buhen.

Principal inscription:

The northern boundary belonging to the land granted to the first prophet of.............arable lands of five arouras in the district of Perwaḥwedja.

553 Inscriptions from the Tomb of the Scribe and Accountant of Grain of Amun, Zeserkarē'seneb, in Western Thebes, No.38.

(Scheill *Mém. Miss.* V 571 ff; Kuentz *BIFAO* 21, 119 ff. coll.)

Zeserkarē'seneb and his family make offering:

Offering all good and pure things and supplying the
braziers with incense and fowl/ to Amun, lord of the thrones 16
of the Two Lands, to Rē'-Ḥarakḥty, to Osiris, ruler of eternity and to Hathor, mistress of the desert, by the grain accointant of Amun, steward and second prophet of Zeserkarē'-seneb, justified.

His "sister", the lady of the house, Wazronpet.

Bringing all (kinds) of fine plants to Amun, lord of the thrones of the Two Lands and to Hathor, mistress of the desert by................

His son, his beloved, the scribe, Meriu.

....

His son, the scribe, Neferḥebef.

His son, the scribe, Neferḥebef.

Zeserkarē'seneb at a feast:

Sitting in a booth in order to enjoy oneself in accordance with one's custom when on earth, by the grain accountant in the granary of the divine offerings of Amun and in the temples which are under the authority of the steward of the second prophet of Amun, Zeserkarē'seneb, justified.

His "sister", his dearly beloved, the lady of the house, Wazronpet, justified, goodly possessor of honour.

Inscription accompanying those who stand in front of them:

His daughter, his beloved, the lady of the house, Nebttaui.

His daughter, his beloved, Merytrē'; she says, For 1639
your ka! Spend a holiday, O scribe and accountant of grain, in your house of justification which you have made for yourself in the area of the City.

Inscription in front of the first daughter:

Partake of a holiday, O accountant of the grain belonging to Amun.

The song of the choir:

> O happy day,
> when men shall call to mind the beauty of Amun
> being glad of heart
> and give praise unto the height of heaven
> before you
> each time that hearts tell concerning what they
> have seen.
> Do it, O grain accountant who belongs to Amun!!

Another offering scene:

Making offering and presenting ab oblation, the body being pure and the fingers clean, and supplying the braziers, with bulls upon the altars, wine and š'yt-cakes for Amun in every dwelling of his, by the accountant of the grain belonging to Amun, and steward of the second prophet of Amun, Zeserka.

The name of an offering bearer:

The keeper of the storehouse of Amun, king of the gods.

Offerings are made to Amun and to Renenutet: 164

Amun, beneficent of designs and Renenutet, the lady of the granary. Offering all good and pure things to Amun in every dwelling of his, by the grain accountant belonging to Amun, Zeserkarē', on this day of measuring out the flour in month four of winter, day twentyseven in the new land of Amun, called Ḥenutseḥerkeḥ.

The speech of an offering bearer:

He says, "for your ka, a bouquet of Amun in Djeserdjeseru."

554 Stela of the Royal Herald Rē', now in Munich

(Dyroff-Pörtner, Süddeutsche Sammlung II pl.13, No. 20.)

An offering which the king gives to Osiris, foremost of westerners that he may grant bread and beer, oxen and fowl, clothing and incense to the ka of the royal herald, Rē'. Made by his brother Parennūfer.

555 Funerary Cone of Rē'

(Mém. Miss.VIII, p.291, No. 198.)

The Osiris, the royal herald of the lord of the Two Lands, praised one of the good god and excellent confidant, Rē'.

556 Stela of Ithu-Wesir re-used in the Mortuary Temple of Tuthmosis IV, now in the Ashmolean Museum, Oxford 1641

(Petrie, Six Temples pl.9, 1; coll.)

An offering which the king gives to Osiris, foremost of westerners, the great god, lord of the hallowed land, that he may grant invocation offerings of bread and beer, oxen and fowl, clothing, alabaster, incense and oil, a thousand of all good and pure things, offerings and sustenance, gifts and all (kinds of) flowers, which the sky gives and the earth creates and which the Nile brings forth from his cavern, the sweet breath of the north wind; (also) to drink water at the river-eddy, to the ka of the escort of his lord upon water, upon land in the southern and northern foreign countries, the restrainer of the territories of the Fenkhu, he who has subdued all who rebel against the king in the land of Retjenu and confidant of the good god, Ithu-Wesir. He says: "O you living upon earth, all w'ab priests, all scribes and all lector priests who shall see this image, the likeness and heir upon earth, remember..............."

Inscription in front of the son:

It is his son, his beloved, who causes his name to live, the stablemaster of the lord of the Two Lands, Minmosi, repeating life, possessor of honour.

557 Inscriptions in the Tomb of the Royal Priest, Dhoutmosi, No. 248 in Western Thebes. 1642

(Transcribed by Helck)

Inscription accompanying the image of the couple:

A feast:

(a) The offerer of Menkheperurē', Ḏḥoutmosi, justified with the great god, lord of eternity. The Osiris, the w'ab priest of 'Akheperurē', Kha'emneter, justified with the great god, lord of eternity.

The w'ab priest of the king's mother, Isis, Mery, justified.

The Osiris, the w'ab priest of 'Akheperkarē', Nakht, justified with the great god.

The Osiris, Akhes-iu.........justified.

The Osiris, the attendant of Menkheperurē', Kha'-emweset, justified with the great god, lord of eternity.

(b) The Osiris, the offerer of Menkheperurē', Ḏḥoutmosi, justified with the great god, lord of eternity.

The Osiris, the lady of the house, Tamert, justified.

You present good and pure (things) for your ka, O offerer.

Inscription below:

An offering which the king gives: all good and pure things, bread and beer, oxen and fowl (for) the lady of the house, Taiunet, justified with the great god, lord of eternity.

The Osiris, Tatu.

558 Inscriptions in the Tomb of the Scribe of the Prince, Menkheper, No. 258 in Western Thebes

(Transcribed by Helck)

Inscription accompanying the image of the couple:

For your ka, O royal protegé, scribe............ Menkheper of the house of the royal princes.

His mother, the lady of the house, praised one of 1
Ḥatḥor, Nay.

Offering prayer:

Giving praise to Osiris and kissing the ground before Wennefer, by the royal protegé and royal scribe, Menkheper, of the house of the royal princes. He says: I give praise to you, that I may extol you and propitiate you in all your names. Hail, Osiris, foremost of westerners and all gods of the hallowed land. Listen to me when I call to you, incline your heart to my need, for there is no god who forgets that which he has created, because your breath of life has entered into my body and your sweet north wind into my heart. It is upon the right road that I have come...........the heart, in order that all my limbs may be made whole, then my soul shall be divine............my name is excellent...........in the mouth of men.....

559 Members of the Family of the Owner of Tomb No. 62 in Western Thebes, the superintendent of the Audience Chamber, Amenemwaskhet 1644

(Transcribed by Helck)

(a) Name of the owner of the tomb on the ceiling:

.............the count, sealbearer of the king of Lower Egypt and superintendent of the audience chamber, Amenemwaskhet, justified.

(b) A feast:

His brother, the w'ab priest of Heliopolis* (?).... ......'ankh...........

His brother................

The w'ab priest of the temple of the Ennead, 'Akheperurē'seneb.

The scribe and confidant of the lord in all his affairs, Mersurē'

The scribe who built this tomb............

Footnote to 559

1644.7 This town could also be Iunet (Denderah), Iuni (Armant),or Iunyt (Latopolis/Esna.)

560 Statue of the Superintendent of the Cattle of Onuris, Meryty, from the Temple of Mut in Karnak, Cairo 916

(Benson-Gourlay *Temple of Mut*, p.330. Borchardt *Statuen III, 152.*)

Cartouche on the right shoulder:

Menkheperurē',(followed by group representing Nekhbet).

Cartouche on the left shoulder:

Tuthmosis, gleaming-of-diadems, (followed by group representing Wadjet.)

Inscription on the front:

An offering which the king gives to Amun-Rē', lord of the thrones of the Two Lands, to Mut, lady of Isheru and to the Ennead of Karnak for the ka of the prince and count, the royal scribe, Meryty, repeating life.

Inscription on the right:

The superintendent of the cattle of Meryty. 16

Inscription on the left:

The guardian of Amun, Meryty.

Inscription on the back:

The master of ceremonies of Osiris, Meryty.

561 Stela of the Necropolis Worker Kha', now in the British Museum

(*Hierogl. Texts* VIII, pl.45, No. 1515.)

Description: Material: limestone.

The device of winged disc and uraei at the head of the stela shows no unusual features. The scene below shows a king (right) offering incense and flowers to Amun-Rē', who is seated on the left.

Inscription:

The good god, lord of the Two Lands, Menkheperurē' son of Rē', Dhoutmosi, given life like Rē' for ever. Beloved of Amun-Rē', lord of the thrones of the Two Lands. May he grant all life, stability and dominion like Rē'.

The god's wife, 'Aḥmosi-nefertere.

Principal inscription:

Giving praise to Amun, kissing the ground before the gods on behalf of the life, prosperity and health of the king of Upper and Lower Egypt. "May you give to him an eternity in joy and an infinity as king of the living", says the stablemaster of the great place, Kha', repeating life, and the servant woman of the god's wife in the Place of Truth, Ḥenutḏu.

Emendations provided by Professor Helck

1541.1–17 Compare D. Müller, ZÄS 84. 158 ff.

1554.1 .....  .....

1555.12  .....

1565.10 This should probably read:

 ......

1567.15 Ḥatḥor 

1576.3 ff. A – see Davies-Macadam, Corpus # 159 where the name has been miscopied as 

B – missing in Davies-Macadam loc. cit.

C – see Davies-Macadam loc. cit # 98

The group  remains.

D – see Davies-Macadam loc. cit #102

where  mn'-nswt is correctly written

1587.17 According to Brunner OLZ 1958 220.2

 should read: 

1591.17 The group 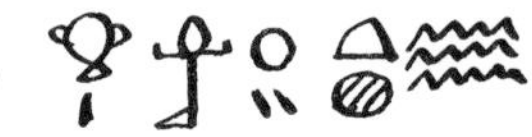 should read: 

19 The group at the end of the line should read: .... 

1593.16 The first group should read:

 ......

1599.17 This line should read:

.19 In this line and in the titles in lines 1600.1/14, 1601.13 the name 'Imn-m-ḥb shou' ' be emended to Ptḥ-m-ḥ3t

1601.16 Ignore the word "gleichen" – "same" in the title

1621.18 The group 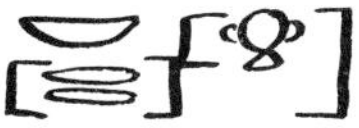 should read: 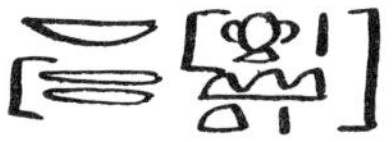 .....

1622.16 The missing group at the beginning of the line is 

1626.19 The group 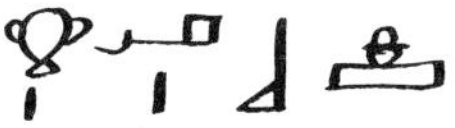 should read: 

1629.11 Emend the first verb to pr.tw n.i

16. According to Davies-Macadam, <u>Corpus</u> #398 this inscription should read: 

19. See Davies-Macadam loc. cit #57

1632.8  should read 
= ḳrst nfrt

1635.12 ff Habib Habachi, Lexikon der Ägyptologie II 637 note 58 attributes this stela to the viceroy Amenḥotp in the reign of Tutankh-amun.

1639.13 The group  should read  . . . . . .

1640.17 See Davies - Macadam Corpus # 466

1641 16 The group  should rather read 

1643.7 The group  should read 

.8 The missing group is 

1643.14 The phrase 
should rather read: 
 .....

.17 The group  should read:

LIST OF ABBREVIATIONS

1. Ann. Serv.

   Annales du Service des Antiquites de L'Égypte, Vol.I. (1900 to present day.)

2. Atlas

   Wreszinsky - Atlas zur Altägyptischen Kulturgeschichte, Leipzig 1936.

3. Berl. Inschr.

   G. Roeder. Äegyptische Inschriften aus den Königlichen. Museen zu Berlin. Leipzig 1913 - 1914.

4. Bifao

   Bulletin de l'Institut Français d'Archeologie Orientale (du Caire), Vol.1. 1901 onwards.

5. Bull.Inst. Franç

   Bulletin de l'Institut Française d'Archeologie Orientale. Cairo 1901 - 1948.

6. Cat. Mon.

   J. de Morgan & others. Catalogue des Monuments et Inscriptions de l'Égypte Antique. Vienna 1894.

7. Denkm.

   Lepsius. Denkmäle aus Ägypten und Äthiopien. Vols.1 - XII. Berlin 1849 - 1858.

LIST OF ABBREVIATIONS Contd.

8. Dict. géog.

Gauthier, Dictionnaire des Noms géographiques.

9. Egypt Inscript

Sharpe. Egyptian Inscriptions from the British Museum and other sources. London, Moxon 1837 - 1955.

10. Gard. AEO

A. H. Gardiner. Ancient Egyptian Onomastica. 3 vols. Oxford University Press 1947.

11. Gard. EG

A. H. Gardiner, Egyptian Grammar. Oxford University Press 1927.

12. Hierogl. Texts

Hieroglyphic Texts from Egyptian Stelae etc. in the British Museum. 8 vols. London 1911 - 1939.

13. Inscr.

Piehl. Inscriptions Hiéroglyphiques Recuellies en Europe et en Égypte. Stockholm - Leipzig 1886 - 1895.

14. Inscript. hiérogl.

De Rougé. Inscriptions hiéroglyphiques copiées en Égypte, pendant la mission scientifique. Paris Vieweg 1877 - 1879.

15. JEA

Journal of Egyptian Archaeology London. Egypt Exploration Society 1914 to present day.

16. LEM

Caminos. Late Egyptian Miscellanies, London. Oxford University Press 1954.

17. MDIK

Mitteilungen des deutshen Instituts für aegyptische Altertumskunde in Cairo. Berlin 1930 - 1944. Wiesbaden 1956.

18. Mém. miss

Mémoires publiés par les membres de la Mission archeologique française du Caire.

19. MDOG

Mitteilungen der deutschen Orient Gesellschaft zu Berlin. Berlin 1899.

20. Not. descr.

Champollion. Monuments de l'Égypte et de la Nubie. Notices descriptives.

21. PSBA

Proceedings of the Society of Biblical Archaeology. London 1879 - 1918.

22. PT

Sethe. *Die ältagyptischen Pyramidentexte* Leipzig 1908 - 1922.

23. Rec. Trav.

Recueil de Travaux Relatifs à la Philologie et à l'Archeologie Egyptiennes et Assyriennes. 40 vols. Paris 1870 - 1923.

24. Statuen

Borchardt. *Statuen und Statuetten von Königen und Privatleuten.* Parts 1 - 5. *Catalogue generale Musee de Caire.*

25. Statues

Legrain. *Statues et Statuettes de Rois et de Particuliers* 3 vols. and index 1906, 1909, 1914 and 1925. *Catalogue generale Musée de Caire.*

26. Stelen

Hermann. *Stelen der Thebanischen Felsgräber der 18 Dynastie*

27. Übersetzung

Helck. *Urkunden der 18 Dynastie Übersetzung zu den Heften 17 - 22.* Akademie Verlag Berlin 1961.

28. Urk

Sethe and Helck. *Urkunden der 18 Dynastie.* Akademie Verlag Berlin.

29. WB

Erman and Grapow. Wörterbuch der Ägyptischen Sprache, 5 vols. Leipzig 1926 - 1931.

30. ZA

Zeitschrift für Assyriologie und Verwandte Gebiete Leipzig 1886 to present day.

31. ZÄS

Zeitschrift für Ägyptische Sprache. Vol. 1863 to present day. Berlin and Leipzig.

GEOGRAPHICAL GLOSSARY

'Ankh-Tawy
A name of Memphis.
(Gauthier Dict.géog.1 149.
Gardiner AEO II 123*)

Antinoe
In Egyptian Ḥer-wer. A town near to Hermopolis.
(Gardiner AEO II 84*)

Armant
In Egyptian Ḏrty. Hermonthis, 20 miles south of Thebes, opposite Tod.
(Gardiner AEO II 21*)

Behḍet
The present-day Edfu.
(Gardiner AEO II 6* ff.)

Buhen
The present-day Wâdy Halfa below the Second Cataract.

Fenkhu
A Syrian people. The earliest mention of them is in the 5th Dynasty temple of Neuserrē'. Sethe ZÄS 45, p.140. Also (Gardiner Notes to Sinuhe p.85 n.1.)

Gerses
A Sudanese locality.
(Gauthier Dict.géog.Vol.V, p.214.)

Ḥesret
Probably the Hermopolitan necropolis.
(Gauthier Dict.géog. IV 42.)

Ḥetepet
A region near Heliopolis.
(Gauthier Dict.géog.IV 145.)

Isheru
The precinct of Mut to the south of Karnak.

Kadesh
A large city on the Orontes, strategically important since it was at the northern end of the valley El-Bika' between Lebanon and Anti-Lebanon.
(Gardiner AEO 1, p.137*)

Kher-'ah'a
In Greek Babylon. A town in which the Ennead was worshipped. Now Old Cairo.
(Gardiner AEO II 131*)

Khor
Syria.
(Gardiner AEO 1 180*)

Kurja
A southern frontier of the empire at Napata.

Kush
At this time a term for an administrative province to the south of the Second Cataract.
(Helck, Kush IV, p.39 ff.)

Mi'am
Aniba. A fortress and important town between the First and Second Cataract.
(Breasted Ancient Records IV, 474 ff.)

Miu
A Sudanese area, the most southerly part of Kush. It occurs in the Karnak list of the southern conquests of Tuthmosis III.
(Gauther Dict. géog. Vol.III, p.11.)

Naharin
Another name for the kingdom of Mittani.

Neferusy
A town near to Hermopolis but further to the north.
(Gardiner AEO II, p.83*)

Retjenu
Part of Syria.
(Gardiner AEO 1, 142*)

Sako
Probably the modern El-Kês in Middle Egypt on the west bank about 15 km. south west of Oxyrhynchus.
(Gardiner AEO 11, 98*?

Sehêl
An island just to the south of Elephantine.
(Gardiner AEO II, 195*)

Senmut
The fortress at Bigeh near the First Cataract.
(Gardiner AEO II, 1*)

Shedet
Now Medinet el-Fayum. Capital of the Fayum in the 21st Upper Egyptian nome.
(Gardiner AEO II, 116*)

Shetyt
The shrine of Sokar in Memphis.

Sile
In Egyptian Tjel. The eastern frontier of Egypt.
(Gardiner AEO II, 202*)

Tekhsy
An area to the south of Kadesh on the Orontes and west of Upi. (Edel ZA 16, 257 and Gardiner AEO II 273*)

Thinis
Capital of the Eighth Upper Egyptian Nome near to Abydos. Exact site unknown. (Gardiner AEO II, 38*)

Tunip
A town on the Orontes to the north of Kadesh. (Gardiner AEO 1, 179*)

Wawat
At this time a name for that part of Nubia between the First and Second Cataracts. (Gardiner AEO 1, p.74* and Dixon JEA 44, 119.)

INDEX NOTES

In the case of private persons and lesser royalty an underlined three-figure reference indicates that the text belongs principally to that person.

An asterisk alone against a place name indicates that it can also be found in the geographical glossary. An asterisk and a line reference point the reader to an appropriate footnote.

1. Divinities

2. Royalty

3. Private Persons and Lesser Royalty

4. Place names. (a) In appropriate cases the transliteration of the name is also given. (b) This list also includes some nationalities and the names of certain buildings.

5. Occupations

DIVINITIES

Amun (Amun-Rē')
On stela from mortuary temple of Tuthmosis IV, 1556

Atum
On stela of Tuthmosis IV from Seriaqus, 1562
Hymn, 1603

Bata
1567

Dedwen
On rock stela of Tuthmosis IV from Konosso, 1555

Fen goddess
1593, 1594, 1605/1607

Field of Reeds
1627, 2098

Horus
On boundary stela of Tuthmosis IV from Wadi Haifa, 1637

Isis
On stela of Amenḥotp, 1636

Ius'as 1631

Khepery
1542, 1544

Ma'ēt 1540

Month
Speech to Tuthmosis IV on his chariot 1560

Mut
1562

Nekhbet 1547

Nepri 1582

Osiris
On stela of Amenḥotp 1616
On stela of Iunna 1630
On stela of Neby 1634
Hymn 1643

Ptah
On stela of Tuthmosis IV from Memphis 1563

Ptah-Sokar
Offerings to 1625,1629

Rē'
Hymn of Nakht 1603
Hymn of Meryrē' 1614
Hymn of Amenḥotp 1635

Rē'-Ḥarakhty
On stela of Tuthmosis IV from Seriaqus 1562

Rē'-Ḥarakhty contd.
In tomb of Nebamun 1621

Rē'-Ḥarmachis 1544

Renenutet
In tomb of Nebamun 1625

Satis 1566

Sepa 1631

Thoth
Speech on architrave in temple of Amada 1568

Wepwawet
On stela of Amenḥotp 1616

ROYALTY

'Akheperurē' 1575

Amenophis II
- Receives offering from Mery 1570
- Served by Haremhab 1589
- Theban tomb, cartouche in 1602

Amenophis III
- Served by Ḥaremḥab 1589
- Name and titles in tomb of Nebamūn 1625

Khafrē'
- On Sphinx Stela of Tuthmosis IV 1544

Tuthmosis IV
- "Dream stela" 1539 (a) foll.
- Nubian campaign of year 8, 1545 foll.
- Name and titles on Lateran obelisk 1548 foll.
- Offering list in Karnak 1553 foll.
- Name and titles from rock stela at Konosso 1555
- Stelae from mortuary temple 1556
- Inscription on fourth pylon, Karnak 1557
- Names and titles on chariot with lists of foreign peoples 1559, 1560
- Names and titles on various smaller objects 1560, 1563
- Monuments from Sinai with regnal year 1564
- Mentioned in monuments of mother 1564
- Dedicatory inscriptions from Karnak 1565
- Titles in Amada 1566 foll.
- Scarabs 1569
- His sons in tomb of Ḥeḳerneḥeḥ 1572, 1573
- Pictures of statuettes in tomb of Thenuna 1581
- Name and titles in tomb of Ḥaremḥab 1589
- Cartouche in tomb 116 in Western Thebes 1602

Tuthmosis IV contd.

Estate dedicated to service of his statue 1611
Names and titles on stela of Neferḥēt 1612
Names and titles on palette of Meryrē' 1615
Adored and receives tribute from Nebamūn 1619
Names and titles from mortuary temple 1632, 1633
Names and titles on rock stela and stela of Neby 1634, 1635
Names and titles on Wadi Halfa boundary stela 1637
Cartouche on stela of Mryty 1644
Names and titles on stela of Kha' 1645

PRIVATE PERSONS AND LESSER ROYALTY

'Aḥmosi-Nefertere 1645

'Akheperure'Seneb 1644

Amenemḥab (Kyky)
525
526

Amenemḥēt I 1573
Amenemḥēt II 1593
Amenemḥēt III 1634

Amenemopēt (f) 1591

Amenemopēt (m) 1604

Amenemwaskhet I 1608
Amenemwaskhet II
559

Amenḥotp I 1573, 1575
Amenḥotp II 1593
Amenḥotp III
539
Amenḥotp IV
549
550
551

'Ankh 1644

Denreg 1633

D̲ḥout 1583

D̲ḥutmosi I
513
D̲ḥutmosi II
537
D̲ḥutmosi III 1642

D̲ḥutnūfer I
531
D̲ḥutnūfer II 1624

Haremḥab I 1634
Ḥaremḥab II
522
523

Ḥaty 1616

Ḥeḳerneḥeḥ
512
514
515

Ḥekreshu 1572, 1575

Ḥenut 1616

Ḥenutḍu 1645

Ḥepu
516

Ḥumasha 1630

Ḥunayt 1571

Ipy
545

Isis 1591

Ithu-Wesir
556

Ithuy 1596

Iunna
544

Iuny 1619

Kaemwēset 1633

Kap 1586, 1588

Kay 1607

Ḳenna 1616

Kha' I 1609
Kha' II
561

Kha'emneter 1642

Kha'emwēset I 1633
Kha'emwēset II 1642

Kha'ut
532

Mana 1620

Meniu 1638

Menkheper
558

Menna I 1583
Menna II
530

Menui 1597

Mery I
511
Mery II 1642

Mereṭhor 1634

Meretseger 1633

Mersurē' 1644

Meryrē'
536
537
538

Meryt I 1583
Meryt II 1586, 1588

Merytrē' 1638

Meryty
560

Min 1583, 1584, 1585

Minmosi 1641

My 1571

Nakht I
528
Nakht II 1642

Nebamūn
540
541
542
543

Nebsen 1601

Nebtes 1630

Nebttaui I 1581
Nebttaui II 1634
Nebttaui III 1638

Neby
548

Neferḥebef 1638

Neferḥēt
533
534

Nefertere 1562

Nehem'away
529

Nehem'awayt 1608

Nezem 1601

Nubmutes 1613

Parennūfer 1640

Paser I 1583
Paser II 1601

Piay 1633

Ptaḥemhēt 1599

Ptaḥmosi 1583

Rē' I 1575
Rē' II
534
535

Ry 1616

Sebekḥotp I
518
519
Sebekḥotp II
520
521

Segerttaui 1623

Senisenbut 1623

Si 1609

Ta'at 1613

Taiunet 1642

Tamert 1642

Tathuia 1634

Tatu 1642

Taui 1603

Tausert 1634

Tentamentet 1607

Teri I 1620
Teri II 1621

Teye 1622

Thenuna
517

Thuna
535

Thunena 1615

Ti'a
505 1564, 1581

Tuna 1613

Turo 1629

Wazet I 1555
Waset II 1564

Wazronpet 1638

Wepwawetmosi 1597

Weret	1623, 1624	Zeserkarē' seneb 523

PLACE NAMES

'A-bau 1618

Abydos 1589. 1611, 1612, 1613, 1616, 1629

Ankh-Tawy* 1567

Antinoë 1631

Armant* 1546, 1566, 1631, 1633

Baky 1567

Beḥdet* 1547

Buhen* 1566, 1636, 1637

Canal of Sebek 1583

Chemmis 1541

Elephantine 1566

El-Kab 1547, 1566

Fayûm 1586, 1587, 1588

Fenkhu* 1560, 1641

Gerses* 1560

Ḥenutesḥerḳeḥ 1640

Hermopolis 1631

Ḥesret* 1615

Ḥetepet* 1631

Intet 1567

Isheru* 1575, 1644

Kadesh* 1560

Kadjar 1556

Karnak 1545,1549,1550, 1552,1557,1571, 1592.

Kher-'aha* 1542

Khor* 1556

Kurja* 1560,1617,1628

Kush* 1556,1568,1592, 1635,1636.

M'am* 1567

Memphis 1542,1585,1631

Miw* 1560

Naharin* 1554,1560,1597, 1617,1620,1628

Neferusy* 1631

PLACE NAMES Contd.

Perwaḥwedja 1637

Retjenu* 1570

Sako* 1567

Sehêl* 1566

Senmut* 1567

Shedet* 1564,1583, 1584, 1587,1588, 1632

Shetyt* 1487,1625, 1629

Sile* 1634,1635

Southern Canal 1583

Tekhsy* 1560

Thebes 1548,1549,1550, 1560,1563,1569, 1589,1595,1604, 1621,1624,1629, 1631,1633.

Thinis* 1631

Tiurek 1560

Tjembu* 1618

Tunip 1560

Two Knives (lake of) 1603

Wadi Halfa (boundary stela) 1637

Wawat* 1545,1635

OCCUPATIONS

Attendant
1579, 1586, 1598, 1617, 1642

Attendant in Privy Council
1577

Attendant of lord of the Two Lands
1587, 1595, 1619, 1620, 1621

Chantress of Amun
1596, 1603, 1604, 1605, 1606, 1609

Chantress of Onuris
1616

Charioteer
1616

Chief of Police (ḥry mḏ3y)
1618, 1620, 1621, 1629

Chief of Police (wr n mḏ3y)
1598, 1634, 1635

Chief Treasurer
1577, 1582, 1583, 1584, 1586.

Commander of Fleet
1618

Confidant of Kush
1636

Crowned prince
1635

District Superintendent
1583

Educator
1572

Eyes and ears of Horus, the King
1595, 1596

Eyes of king of Upper Egypt and ears of king of Lower Egypt
1579, 1580, 1599, 1628.

Eyes of king
1608

Fanbearer
1574, 1579, 1584, 1595, 1613, 1635.

Father of the God
1572, 1574, 1575

Father and beloved of the God
1576, 1581

Father of the God and beloved of the God
1574, 1582

Father of the God belonging to the great throne
1571

Favourite of the king
1579, 1582, 1587, 1593, 1599, 1607, 1613.

First prophet of Amun
1570, 1571.

First prophet of Menkheperurē'
1633

OCCUPATIONS Contd.

First prophet of Month
1633

First prophet of the moon
1583

First prophet of Onuris
1616, 1617

First royal herald
1575

Goldsmith
1607

Grain accountant
1597, 1638, 1639, 1640

Great chief spokesman
1578

Great royal wife
1581

Guardian of Amun
1645

High steward
1580, 1581, 1614, 1615

Lady of house
1571, 1586, 1588, 1595, 1596, 1605, 1606, 1609, 1613, 1616, 1622, 1623, 1630, 1633, 1634, 1638, 1642

Lector priest
1588, 1641

Majordomo
1577

Master of ceremonies
1614, 1645

Master craftsman
1611, 1631, 1632

Master craftsman of the Neshmet barque
1630

Master and governor of Upper Egypt
1571

Mayor
1588

Mayor of the Fayûm
1586, 1587

Mayor of Lake of Sebek
1583, 1584, 1586

Mayor of Southern Canal of Sebek
1583

Mayor of Sile
1634, 1635

Mayor of Southern lake and Northern lake
1588

Nurse
1571, 1583

Offerer
1642

Offering bearer
1583

Police Deputy
1620

Prince
1618

Prince and count
1570, 1571, 1574, 1576, 1578, 1579, 1580, 1581, 1582, 1584, 1586, 1587, 1593, 1595, 1596, 1598, 1600, 1602, 1613, 1614, 1615, 1619, 1621, 1623, 1628, 1635, 1644

Prince of Min and Isis
1538

Prophet
1610

Prophet of Great of Magic
1574

Prophet of Sebek
1583

Real royal scribe
1595, 1596, 1610

Representative of his Majesty
1522

Royal favourite
1586, 1608, 1623

Royal Herald
1640

Royal messenger
1634

Royal scribe
1592, 1595, 1596, 1597, 1610, 1619, 1635, 1636, 1637, 1643, 1644

Royal scribe of recruits
1513

Scribe of arable lands
1609

Scribe of estate of Menkheperurē'
1633

Scribe of recruits
1596, 1597

Scribe of royal steward
1615

Scribe of the treasury
1513, 1514

Sculptor
1607

Sealbearer of king of Lower Egypt
1571, 1579, 1581, 1582, 1613, 1614, 1636, 1644

Second prophet of Amun
1638

Servant of the God's wife
1645

Skywatcher
1603, 1604, 1605, 1606

Sole companion
1577, 1579, 1613, 1614

Stablemaster
1617, 1637, 1641, 1645

Standard bearer
1618, 1619, 1620, 1621, 1622, 1623, 1624, 1625, 1627, 1629

Steward of the harim of the queen
1634

Steward of Month
1633

Steward of private chamber of Pharoah
1592

Steward of the second prophet of Amun
1639

Superintendent of all royal scribes of the army
1596

Superintendent of arable lands
1571, 1596, 1608, 1609

Superintendent of audience chamber
1644

Superintendent of calves, cows and bulls of Amun
1596

Superintendent of cattle
1581, 1586, 1594, 1633, 1635, 1636, 1637, 1645

Superintendent of the City
1576, 1577

Superintendent of deserts of Western Thebes
1535, 1539, 1629

Superintendent and director of Upper and Lower Egypt
1514

Superintendent of fortresses of land of Wawat
1635

Superintendent of feathered and scaly animals
1596

Superintendent of horned animals
1596

Superintendent of horses
1576, 1596, 1599

Superintendent of two houses of silver
1571

Superintendent of two houses of gold and two houses of silver
1614

Superintendent of law courts
1576

Superintendent of marshlands
1586, 1587

Superintendent of marshy lake
1636

Superintendent of ploughlands
1608

Superintendent of prophets
1633

Superintendent of prophets of Upper and Lower Egypt
1570, 1571, 1594, 1596

Superintendent of prophets of Sebek
1583, 1586, 1587, 1588

Superintendent of ships
1632

Superintendent of treasury
1582

Superintendent of works
1586, 1596, 1612, 1613, 1637

Troop captain
1592, 1593, 1598, 1624, 1634, 1635

Tutor
1572, 1574, 1575, 1576

Veteran of army
1619

Viceroy
1635, 1636, 1637

Vizier
1576, 1577

W'ab priest
1588, 1609, 1611, 1642, 1644